**Reiki** *Practical ways to harmony*

# Reiki

practical
ways to
harmony

## MARI HALL

Thorsons

*To all people who remember that we are one family, one spirit.*

Thorsons
An Imprint of HarperCollins*Publishers*
77–85 Fulham Palace Road,
Hammersmith, London W6 8JB

The Thorsons website address is
www.thorsons.com

First published by Thorsons 1997 as *Practical Reiki*
This edition published by Thorsons 2000

10 9 8 7 6 5 4 3 2 1

Text Copyright © Mari Hall 1997, 2000
Copyright © HarperCollins *Publishers* Ltd 2000

Designer: Jo Ridgeway
Editor: Nicky Vimpany
Photography: Henry Allen
Illustrations by Jane Spencer

Mari Hall asserts the moral right to
be identified as the author of this work

A catalogue record for this book
is available from the British Library

ISBN 0 00 710124 4

Printed in Hong Kong

# Contents

# Acknowledgements

It is my heartfelt joy to acknowledge:

My many students and clients who have walked beside me and allowed me to be a silent witness to their miracles.

K. Bradford Brown and J. Roy Whitten, co-founders of 'The Life Training', who taught me to listen to my mind, feel with my heart and, most importantly, to live LIFE fully.

The publishers wish to thank Tanny Smith, Stephanie Hill, Nick Williams and Helen Bee for modelling for this book.

# An Important Foreword

To give first or second degree Reiki, or to be a Reiki practitioner or Master of Reiki, requires that you receive attunements *in person* from a Reiki Master Teacher who has themselves received the attunements and training. This book can never be regarded as a substitute for that direct initiation process.

It was written to be informative, with the express desire to give you an understanding of Reiki and how it can be used, and to open up to you the possibility that you too could be an instrument for this loving energy. Once you have been initiated by a Reiki Master who has been properly trained, this book can be used as a guide for you to do your work.

# Introduction

You are about to begin a special journey as you read this book. It is my hope that it will awaken you to the possibility that you can also reach out and help, people or yourself, and be touched by one of the highest forms of energy that exists. Reiki originated in Tibet over 3,000 years ago and has been passed down through the centuries. It is not hard to learn: in fact, Reiki is the simplest therapeutic method I know of. It possesses a unique wisdom of its own, directing itself to where it is most needed. No special medical knowledge is necessary in order to practise Reiki. It can be used to complement all other healing methods. It is simple to use – all you need is your hands to transfer this energy. Often immediate relief is obtained for all kinds of complaints. It has been my experience that the healing and harmonizing effects of Reiki involve not only the recipient, but the instrument (the person giving the Reiki) as well, leaving them both filled with peace, joy and vitality.

When I first became a Reiki Master, I wrote manuals for my students to use in the seminars. It was very important to me that the manuals should contain the purest essence of Reiki and be presented with integrity. I spent months compiling the information and writing the text. Each manual is an integral part of the Reiki courses I teach. As time has gone by, I have changed, and the manuals have changed too. They have undergone three major revisions. The pure essence of Reiki is still there, supplemented by other information I have come across and found useful. The latest material from my course manuals is included in this book. The history of Reiki that is found in Chapter 1 is the one told to me by my Reiki Master; it contains many spiritual principles that have helped me on my

life's journey. *Practical Reiki* was written in the hope that more and more people will know about this wonderful natural healing method. It is my desire that somewhere in these pages, you will be encouraged to take a Reiki course in order to use this technique with your family, friends and yourself, or to have a Reiki treatment. I can truly say that, either way, there is usually a feeling of having experienced something beautiful. Your heart will open and, as a result of this experience, something within will be transformed.

Reiki is not in the mind; it is in the heart. Feeling it is always the greatest teacher.

## ABOUT MYSELF AND MY VISION

A trusted friend and teacher, K. Bradford Brown, asked me many years ago how I wanted the world to be. During a meditation I had a vision for the world. My eyes were closed, yet I could see the world as we might see it from space. All around the world were people holding hands. They were brothers and sisters. We had respect for our differences – all the things that made us the wonderful, unique individuals that we are. It did not matter that we had different skin colours, philosophies and languages, because we had something that overcame all these things and united us. It was LOVE and there was peace in our world.

I realized that, in order to have peace outside of me, it had to start within me first. I began my search for that something that would bring me peace and, hopefully, health. I had been reading about and studying religion and different philosophies, thinking that if I came back to a spiritual centre-point my problems would be solved. I had been awarded a doctorate in divinity, yet my health, both physically and emotionally, was still not good. I was divorced from my husband and had taken a powerful course called 'The Life Training', which had originated in California, in the USA. This had been a big turning point in my life. The training gave me the tools to cease living my life from the conditioned reactions of my mind, and to respond to life with love.

Throughout my early life, I was constantly 'down' with something.

I had all sorts of illnesses. I spent a good part of my married life in and out of hospitals and having major surgery. I heard about Reiki and was ready! I became so convinced that this was my life path that I became a Reiki Master. Over the years, Reiki has deepened my spiritual experience and in 1988 I was ordained as a minister of religion and counsellor. It has given me health and vitality so that I have never since been hospitalized. I travel and teach Reiki to people of many different countries and cultures who are searching for something with meaning in their lives – a way to be active in their own health and in the health of others.

The vision I had many years ago is still alive in me. It is in my mind and heart. It is the motivation to continue my work for world peace with the use of Reiki. I designed a symbol to represent this vision. It is a symbol I wear all the time and I am sharing it with you:

It is called 'The Heart of the Family' and is also the symbol for The International Association of Reiki. The people on the outside of the drawing represent the people all around the world holding hands – the brothers and sisters. The heart represents the love and respect that we have for each other and for ourselves. The baby represents the innocence and purity of our souls – the Light. We are the heart of the family; each of us is important and integral to each other and to our world.

I welcome you to join with us in this vision of a peaceful, love-filled world, starting with ourselves and spreading out to all humanity.

# What is Reiki?

Reiki is a Japanese word and is pronounced 'Ray-Key'.

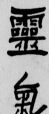 

There are many styles of calligraphy for writing Japanese characters. These are the normal ways to see Reiki written. The first is an actual copy of Hawayo Takata's calligraphy and the other is the style commonly used by the Reiki Alliance (another international organization of Reiki). Both are Japanese calligraphy for Reiki

'Rei' is defined as Universal life giving and, like the rays of the sun, it gives life to living things. It is all-knowing; a spiritual consciousness. 'Ki' is defined as energy: this energy or life force flows through all things that are alive. 'Ki' is also known as Light, Prana, Chi, Cosmic Energy, or Universal Radiant Energy.

Reiki is Universal Life-giving Energy and can be used for all purposes, conditions and situations. It can be safely used at any time, in any place and for anything. To practise Reiki, no faith or belief is required. It is successfully used by people of many different religions, philosophies and ages. It is for everyone. Reiki is the

simplest natural healing method I know of. Once a person is reawakened by a Reiki Master with an initiation process, then the ability to transmit this energy will be theirs for the rest of their lives and will flow through their hands naturally.

It is my belief that we are all born with this Universal Life Energy, but that our reactions to life cause us to become less open, with the result that the natural flow of energy is less pure and less available. Our personality, that is our ego or false self, is the filter for the energy. Practising Reiki can enable us to shift into a harmonious state that is often referred to as an alpha or theta state of consciousness. In these states of being, the filter is harmonized, returning us to our natural wholeness. We are open to the divine moment of love and healing.

## WHAT REIKI IS NOT

Reiki is not mind-directed energy, polarity therapy or therapy using magnetism. With these approaches, the therapist must see the energy coming into them and direct it with their minds. In these approaches to healing, illness is considered as negative energy. The therapist, who is filled with positive energy, attracts the negative energy like a magnet, pulling it away and removing it from the client. One of the biggest fears is that the negative energy from the client will somehow attach itself to the therapist, making them ill. Or conversely, there is concern that, if the therapist has negative energy, it could be picked up by the client.

## WHAT REIKI IS

With Reiki, you do not have to see the energy, nor concentrate on it at all. Nor do you remove energy from someone, or give them your energy. Reiki energy balances and harmonizes. If there is too much energy in an area, or if there is not enough, the area is out of balance: when there is imbalance, there is potential for illness. In a balanced state, the individual has the potential for self-healing. The energy is transmitted simply by placing your hands on yourself or another individual.

We do not diagnose with Reiki. Rather, we understand that the body is in a state of balance or imbalance. Reiki makes its way to the areas of imbalance during a treatment. No medical or diagnostic education is required. Reiki works on many levels. Physical, mental, emotional and spiritual well-being are all enhanced with Reiki energy.

Energy is all around us and inside us as well. We constantly react and respond to energy without realizing it, all day, every day. Around us is an energy field, which is referred to as the aura. The aura has many levels: emotional, mental and spiritual levels. Surrounding the Universe is an aura with layers as well. One of these layers is called Universal, Unconditional Love. Reiki is the Unconditional Love of the Universe. If you are a religious person and believe that God, or Universal divine essence, by whatever name it is called, created the Universe, you can think of Reiki as the Unconditional Love of God or that divine essence.

Reiki is given from the heart and is often experienced as the receiving of unconditional love. This love has the power to bring us back to a state of peace and harmony. This state can be described as health or wholeness. For many people, giving and receiving this energy is a spiritual experience, because we experience 'wholeness', which is holy. It is impossible for me to separate holiness from Reiki. It has been my continued experience as a Reiki Master, an instrument and recipient of this energy, that wholeness is a feeling and expression of 'being one' with all living things.

Illness is the result of imbalance. The cause of the illness can usually be found at a deep emotional, mental or spiritual level. For instance, if you always lived your life in fear, the imbalance could occur in different areas of your body. One is the solar plexus region, as fear usually constricts energy there (producing, for example, a tight, cold stomach). You could also have constricted energy in the throat area, from not expressing yourself. The potential for illness will always be greater in areas of imbalance.

When I was a young girl, a series of incidents happened which influenced me in making a decision not to trust anyone or anything. This was a mental decision that was based on an emotional reaction. As a result, I had chronic throat problems throughout my life. Imbalance created illness. Because the Reiki energy works on all levels, the cause is being treated as well as the resulting illness.

Most importantly, people who transmit Reiki energy are not healers; they are instruments for this energy. The person who receives the energy is harmonized so that their body can heal itself naturally. They are empowered in their healing process. There is a natural relationship, a partnership. The recipient is always the healer.

Also, as you transmit this energy you are being harmonized at the same time. You are receiving a treatment as you are giving one. The more you use Reiki, the better it becomes, because you are becoming more harmonized. The more balanced you are, the better the energy will be.

## UNDERSTANDING REIKI

Reiki cannot be understood with the mind. It is not logical. Although many have tried to demystify it with rational explanations, there remains a mystery that cannot be explained by words, but must be understood through experience. The experience of giving Reiki, once you have been initiated into the system by a Reiki Master, and that of receiving it from one who has been initiated. In this experience you discover such an incredible peace and relaxation that it may seem as though you are transported back to your innate truth, your perfection of body, mind and spirit.

It is probably the safest and yet most effective method of transferring life energy. It requires no specific philosophy or religion. No skill or special preparations or previous degrees are necessary. Anyone can become an instrument for the energy of Reiki in a matter of a day or two. Of course it goes without saying that daily practice will deepen the understanding of this universal life force and will also help you to become a clearer instrument for the energy.

I say instrument because the person who is giving the energy is not actually healing anyone. The energy passes through them to another person, plant or living organism and the receiver of this loving energy heals him or herself by using the energy. I have been blessed as a Reiki instrument and Reiki Master to be a witness to many miracles. I never have any expectation of how Reiki energy will be used. The process of healing is not in my hands; rather I am blessed to be a part of the process, but do not affect it. The perspective is different to traditional healing where the 'Healer' is doing something to the recipient. Reiki treatment is safe in any situation, time or circumstances, irrespective of the disease or discomfort. It is also suitable for professional medical care. It is easily combined with orthodox medicine as well as all alternative therapies.

1

The
Beginning

# A return to wisdom

Imagine that you are sitting on the top of a mountain. It is the twenty-first day of your meditative and fasting practice. You have been praying for enlightenment, for a deeper understanding of how to heal the body. The early morning is dark and, as you throw the last small stone that you have gathered to mark the days, a light suddenly appears from nowhere and streams towards you. The light enters you, and in that moment your prayers are answered, your 21-day quest to understand ends and another exciting journey begins.

It sounds like a fairy tale and yet it is part of the journey undertaken in the Meiji-era in Japan by Mikao Usui to rediscover the ancient hands-on healing method that he named Reiki.

Reiki can be translated into Universal Life Giving Energy. From my own experience, I simply say it is Universal, Unconditional Love or Pure Heart Energy. Reiki energy is a love that has no boundaries and gives us the potential to be the witnesses to miracles in others and ourselves.

There are many stories about Mikao Usui. Recently, a more Eastern version of the story of Usui has surfaced in a book entitled *Reiki Fire* by Frank Petter. Frank and his wife Cheetna desired to become closer to the man who gave us Reiki by visiting his grave site in the Toyotama district in Tokyo, Japan. They have also spoken with the people that continue to uphold Usui's principles in Usui Shiki Ryoho. The original Reiki association *Usui Reiki Ryoho Gakkai* that Usui founded in Tokyo, Japan is still very active today.

Mikao Usui was born on August 15, 1865 in the village of Yago in the Yamagata district in southern Japan to Uzaemon and Kawai Usui. It was the Keio period (*Keio Gunnen*). We are given to understand that he was a talented and hardworking student and as an adult he travelled several times to countries in the West and also to China to study. He was a very dedicated man. He married Sadako Suzuki and had two children: a girl and a boy.

One day he went to Mount Kurama to undertake a 21-day retreat. During this time he fasted and meditated. At the end of this 21-day period he felt an incredible energy enter his head and discovered that he could use his hands to heal various ailments in himself and his family. He had reached a level of understanding and had been given answers in his meditations. He called this energy Reiki. He opened a clinic in Tokyo, Japan in the April of 1921. He gave Reiki treatments to many people who came from far and wide and also started to give workshops to spread his knowledge to others. In 1923 there was a devastating earthquake that shook Tokyo. Thousands of people were killed, injured and became sick in its aftermath. He took Reiki to the devastated city, giving Reiki treatments to the survivors. His clinic became so popular that it was soon too small to handle the amount of people that came to him to experience the healing powers of Reiki. He built a larger clinic outside Tokyo in Nakano in 1924. The Meiji Emperor of Japan honored him for the work he had done with the people of Tokyo after the earthquake. He was called Sensei (Teacher). He was a warm and humble person who always had a smile on his face and never showed off his knowledge. He was simple, honest and very courageous in the face of adversity. The people loved him

and showed great respect for his knowledge and his compassion. During his travels to Fukuyama to work and lecture about Reiki he had a fatal stroke on March 9, 1926. He was 61 years of age and had recovered fully from two previous strokes. He is buried with his wife and son, Fuji Usui, at a Shoji Buddhist temple in the suburbs of Tokyo.

The inscription on the tomb stone on Usui's grave that was put there shortly after his death by a group of his students reads that he taught Reiki to about 2,000 people. There were Reiki centres and Reiki clinics in all parts of the country. Workshops by Usui and his chief disciples were conducted on a regular basis. The inscription on the tombstone goes on as follows

*'Someone who studies hard (i.e. practices meditation) and works very hard to improve body and mind for the sake of becoming a better person is called a man of Great Spirit. People who use that Great Spirit for a soul purpose, that is to teach the right way to many people and do collective good, are called teachers. Dr. Usui was such a teacher. He taught the Reiki of the Universe (universal energy). Countless people came to him and asked him to teach them the great way of Reiki and to heal them.*

*Reiki not only heals diseases, but also amplifies innate abilities, balances the spirit, makes the body healthy, and thus to achieve happiness. To teach this to others you should follow the five principles of the Meiji Emperor and contemplate them daily in your heart.*

*They should be spoken daily, once in the morning and once at night.*

1. *Just for today, do not anger*
2. *Do not worry*
3. *Be filled with gratitude*
4. *Devote yourself to your work*
5. *Be kind to people*

*Even now, after Usui's passing, Reiki will be spread far and wide for a long time to come. It is a Universal Blessing to have received Reiki from Sensei Usui and to be able to pass it on to others. Many of Sensei Usui's students have built this memorial here at Saihoji Temple to honor him. May many understand what a great service Usui did to the world.'* [1]

Little did his students know how insightful their wish was. Reiki now circles the world and has been instrumental in bringing many people of different nationalities and philosophies together in love and brotherhood.

Eventually Reiki was brought to the United States by Hawayo Takata. She was a widow who studied with one of Usui's Reiki teachers, a man named Churijo Hayashi. Takata had come to Japan seeking help for her chronic illness. She was treated in Hayashi's clinic and eventually worked beside him and other therapists as part of her training procedure. After a year she went back to Hawaii where she lived with her two daughters. Hayashi visited her in Hawaii in 1938 and made

her a Reiki Master (Sensei). She eventually brought the message of Reiki to the United States, but only in her seventies did she begin to train Reiki Masters herself. On December 11, 1980 she passed away, leaving 22 Reiki Masters in the USA and Canada. A group of her Reiki Masters formed the Reiki Alliance and elected Takata's granddaughter Phyllis Lei Furumoto as her successor. The Alliance was formed to insure that the knowledge of Reiki was passed on. Some of Takata's Masters did not join the Alliance and choose to be independent of the Alliance. One woman, Barbara Ray founded what is now called the 'Radiance Technique'.

Now, just 20 years later, Reiki has spread like wild fire all over the world. There are many Reiki Masters from many schools or disciplines of Reiki, including the Alliance and independent Masters. Hundreds of thousands of people's lives have been changed as a result of three people's initial dedication to Reiki – Usui, Hayashi and Takata.

1 Frank Arjava Petter, 'Reiki Fire'(Twin Lakes, Wis., Lotus Light, 1997)

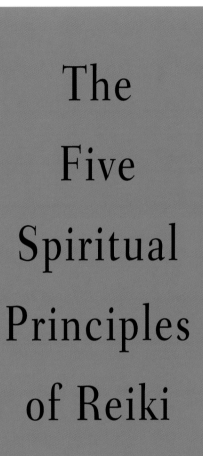

The
Five
Spiritual
Principles
of Reiki

*Just for today, I will let go of anger.*
*Just for today, I will let go of worry.*
*Today, I will count my many blessings.*
*Today, I will do my work honestly.*
*Today, I will be kind to every living creature.*
DR MIKAO USUI

## JUST FOR TODAY, I WILL LET GO OF ANGER.

To let go of anger is to release what is blocking us from loving unconditionally. Anger is really an unnecessary emotion, which separates us from the Universal Consciousness. When our expectations about ourselves and others get the best of us, when we or they fail to satisfy these expectations, or our needs and desires, then we become angry. The people we are angry with usually have no idea that we are angry. Most of the time, it hurts us more than it could ever hurt them. Remember that all beings are brought into our lives as a mirror, and are the direct reflection of the cause and effect created by ourselves. Through the people we bring into our lives, our mirrors, we can discover the weak points in our egos. To be angry is very destructive of our inner harmony. Be aware of what causes the anger – just what is the expectation and/or demand? Feel the emotion fully and release it. Anger is a reaction; the response is love.

*Do not blame others by pointing out their faults.*
*You will find upon self-examination*

*that the faults you see in others are in you.*
*When you correct yourself, the world becomes correct.*
SAI BABA

## JUST FOR TODAY, I WILL LET GO OF WORRY.

When we worry, we have forgotten that there is a divine purpose in everything. When we are aware that we have lived each day the best we can, we know that the rest is up to the Universe. When we worry, we separate ourselves from the Universal wholeness. Also, we are not trusting that all is in divine order. To worry creates more limitations. Surrender to the plan of our higher self. All is in divine order. Release and trust.

*Nothing is cast away by the mind. As*
*a consequence, grief, worry and misery*
*continue to simmer in it.*
*If only the mind can be taught renunciation,*
*one can become a spiritually serene person.*
SAI BABA

## TODAY, I WILL COUNT MY MANY BLESSINGS.

Counting our blessings means being grateful for all the abundance in our lives. We are thankful not only for what we have received, but also for what we know

and trust will be provided. As we acknowledge and give thanks for our every blessing, large and small, we attract more blessings to us. Our fear of not having (lack) keeps us from accepting what is truly ours by divine right. What we are able to see, we shall have; what we think, we shall create. If we feel subconsciously unworthy of receiving abundance or blessings from the Universe, we will in some way block the flow of life's riches and blessings to us. Riches not only in the material sense, but also riches emotionally, mentally and spiritually as well. I see how abundantly I am blessed in my life. All things nourish me and I am grateful.

*To those who have an insight into life,*
*everything has meaning.*
*To those*
*whose eyes are open,*
*everything fits into place.*
SAI BABA

## TODAY, I WILL DO MY WORK HONESTLY.

To live life honestly is to be aligned with our higher self's purpose. By being honest with ourselves and facing the truth in all matters, we can live a truly harmonious life. Truth brings clarity. When we are honest with ourselves, we project honesty onto others. By being honest in our work, this truth is reinforced by the resulting love for ourselves and others. This honesty creates harmony in our

lives and in our world. We complete the task with less effort. As we clearly see and acknowledge the lessons, our life opens before us.

*Truth is your Father*
*Love is your Mother*
*Wisdom your son*
*Peace is your daughter*
*Devotion is your brother*
*and spiritual seekers*
*are your friends.*
SAI BABA

## TODAY, I WILL BE KIND TO EVERY LIVING CREATURE.

As we love and are kind to all living creatures, we experience a sense of unity. We are all of one source. By not being kind to someone we are not loving and respecting ourselves, for we are a part of one another. When we accept all aspects of ourselves, then we can accept others.

*Do not do unto another*
*what you do not like*
*to be done unto yourself.*
*For the other is you.*
SAI BABA

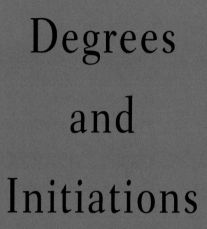

# 3

# Degrees
# and
# Initiations

Many people ask me what sort of Reiki training I would recommend.

The first step is to take a course in Reiki. You start with the first degree of Reiki. During the Reiki One course, the student has four of the spiritual energetic centres (chakras) initiated by the Reiki Master. It is a time of reconnecting to spiritual divinity, a reawakening and attunement to the vibration of Reiki. Once you are initiated, the energy of Reiki is available for the rest of your life.

What I personally found, was that while I thought I would be mastering a technique called Reiki, what actually happened was that I started a journey of being mastered by the energy. In that mastery is the return to wholeness. Every new step I have taken in Reiki has certainly proven this thought true. It becomes a never-ending process of surrender. When we are touched by this energy, part of the coming back into harmony comes from letting go of disharmony, surrendering the parts of us that hold on to what keeps us out of balance. We may not know what these are on a conscious level, and it is not necessary to know. Reiki in its wonderful way finds the aspects that are not harmonized and helps us return to a balanced state.

Taking a Reiki One course is the beginning of the process. It is important to use Reiki in your daily life. We learn best through using Reiki. At some time later a student can decide to take a Reiki Two course. In the second degree course, the student experiences another initiation and learns three ancient symbols that are associated with Reiki. These symbols, together with the initiation, can be used to increase the intensity of the energy. The second degree energy works very deeply on the emotional and mental levels, and the student is taught to send the energy to a distant recipient. You will find that your ability to respond with Reiki is virtually unlimited by time or space. Generally this is all one would need for everyday situations. With first and second degree Reiki you can be an effective instrument for yourself, your family, friends and the community at large.

There are four degrees of Reiki.

## THE FIRST DEGREE

In the first degree, four of your energy centres are reawakened and attuned. The energy centres are known as chakras. At this first level your visionary qualities can become more open, which will help you to experience your soul, that eternal light, and its purpose. You are permanently aligned with love. The first degree attunements are primarily focused on the physical body, so that it can respond by opening up to accept and transfer greater quantities of the life force energy. The attunements will raise the vibratory level of the four spiritual centres:

1   **The initiation of the heart centre awakens you to unconditional love and attunes both the physical heart and the thymus, our 'spiritual heart', as well as attuning the heart chakra on the etheric level.**

2 The initiation of the throat centre awakens the inner being to the aspect of trust and communication. It attunes the thyroid gland and, on the etheric level, the throat chakra.

3 The initiation of the third eye centre awakens the potential for intuition, a deeper knowing and connection to the divine will of this Universal energy that is Reiki. The attunement is on the pituitary gland, which is our centre of intuition and higher consciousness, and the hypothalamus which controls the body's temperature and our moods. The attunement on the etheric level is of the third eye chakra.

4 The initiation of the crown centre aligns you to this higher form of energy, and to spiritual consciousness. It attunes the pineal gland, which is sometimes known as 'the receiver of the light', and attunes the crown chakra on the etheric level.

## THE SECOND DEGREE

In the second degree, you learn absent healing. Reiki Two energy works very deeply on the mental and emotional causes of disease. The second degree places great emphasis on adjusting the etheric rather than the physical body which is the focus of Reiki One. It tends to stimulate the intuitive centre that is located at the pituitary gland – the body's 'telepathic centre'. After the second degree initiation, this centre seems to become sharper and more focused and, as a result of

this process, the Reiki Two students often find themselves more aligned to their Higher Selves.

## THE THIRD DEGREE

In the third degree, the lower energy centres are opened and attuned. This is the first step to becoming a Reiki Master. You begin an apprenticeship programme with a Reiki Master which lasts about two years. The student must be so aligned with the system of Reiki that there is no doubt in their whole being that it is their sole purpose and destiny to become a Master.

Everything you do, everything you say, is an example and demonstration of Reiki. You are living your Reiki. You are Reiki!

## THE FOURTH DEGREE

In the fourth degree, you are initiated as a Reiki Master. Not many people take this path, but once they do, it is a pathway filled with growth and blessings.

I have never regretted my choice to become a Master and have been blessed in my life of service and dedication with the use of Reiki.

## REIKI IS IN US

I believe that Reiki is inherent in all beings. It is something we are born with, which lies dormant within us until it is awakened by a Reiki Master. During the initiation process, an inner healing aspect is reawakened within us, so that we are attuned to the energy of Reiki.

Each person's experience with the initiation is different, because we are all unique individuals. Many people find the experience deeply moving. In some way, their lives are changed and they are never the same afterwards.

*Where love is, great changes and healing take place.*
MARI HALL

I teach a series of other courses that are designed to support the awakened spirit in us all. I have found that the emotions are a large factor in the creation of disharmony. There is a five-day seminar that is designed to help us experience our growth cycles and senses. It puts us in touch with the early decisions and emotions that we have put into place during our growth process, and also gives us the opportunity to release this in a constructive and empowering way.

I also have a nine-month course for students who have done Reiki Two. This is an intensive course that works through the entire chakra system; we meet once a month for the whole weekend. We use a combination of movement, colour,

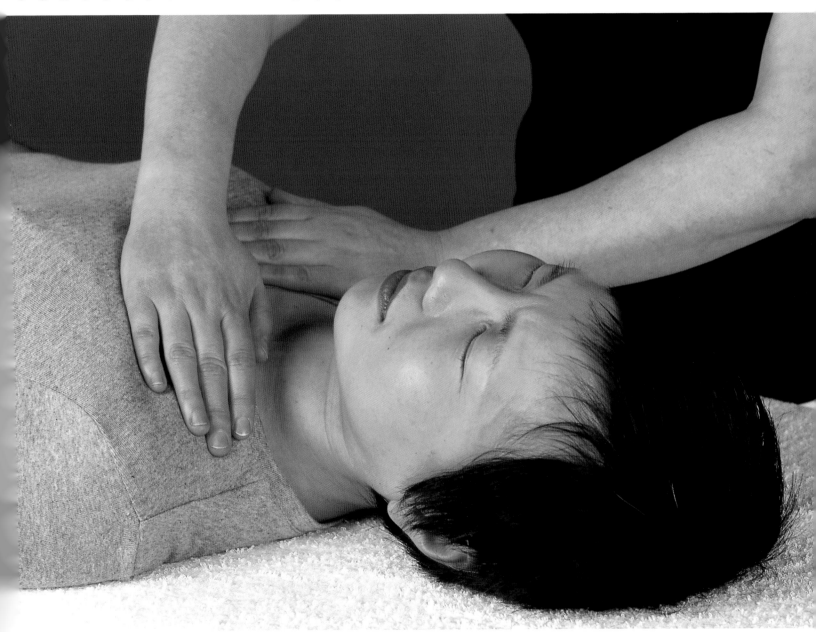

sound, exercise, group and individual work, and we also use the book *Celestine Prophesy* as part of our redefinition process. It is a powerful and moving experience. I have made this course part of the requirement to become a professional Reiki therapist. I firmly believe the more we are willing to understand about ourselves and to discover about our personal shadows, the better we can be as a person working with others. I cannot stress enough that the work starts first with the self.

I love teaching all the courses: each has a special place in my heart and I can see the value in each one, not only for the individual but also for the results that will affect the world through them.

I have introduced the first Reiki Professional Therapist course in the Czech Republic. This is the third level. Several of my students have spent 14 intensive days with me in the mountains near Liberec in the summer, learning about themselves and also how to take Reiki from a household art to a professional therapy. The course includes anatomy, physiology, counselling skills and practice application. It is a beautiful experience.

I have initiated the first Masters through our International Association of Reiki in the Czech Republic. They have devoted at least five to seven years of their lives living their Reiki, working very deeply on themselves and their Reiki practice before starting on their Master journey and a deeper form of surrender. Certainly they have been searching and discovering about themselves for more than this

time, however, the past few years have been intensive and at my side. I believe that the path to Master is one of careful preparation. Building a good foundation for yourself and your work.

There is a certain amount of magic or ritual in all things that we do in our lives. While it is not required, it seems to be human nature that we are drawn to it. I only recently discovered that I put my shoes and socks on in a particular way each day. It is a ritual, part of the way I dress my self.

Giving Reiki to myself every day is a process of touching into my spirit and the spirit of wholeness or Oneness. Like a blessing it serves to start and end my day and is something I look forward to.

In the teaching of Reiki the initiation process is a ritual. A time of Student and Master coming together. I believe the relationship that the student and Master form is a very special one, one that is supporting for both of them. I work very hard at maintaining a realistic relationship that continues to empower the student. I do not have their answers. I can speak out of my own experience, yet I always encourage the student to find their own answers inside themselves. They are the magic. I am not a guru, rather a woman who has life experience that perhaps can help others, I am a Master of Reiki in so much as I continue to be mastered by Reiki. I always remember that as I teach I am also being taught, for all of us are teachers to each other.

I have a policy that I am available to my students and will be as close to them as they will allow. The first principle in our association is that we are a family. As a Reiki family, we are all brothers and sisters. There is a natural exchange of love when we come together. It is quite natural to hug each other hello, to be interested in what each of us are doing and learning and also to support each other. We are living our Reiki together, creating a microcosm, a picture for what the bigger world can choose to experience.

Can you imagine how the world can be in the future if we as a group of people decided that we were brothers and sisters? If we decided that each person has a value, is worth listening to? If we stepped out of what limits us into relationship? Can you imagine how we could live if we communicated and took ownership of how we react and respond? I truly believe this is where we are heading. In the future we can and will live in a peace-filled environment. But, first we must realize that everything we do affects the greater whole. We are not separate. The ego is what separates us. We struggle so hard to define ourselves and create space around us as individuals, forgetting that we can be individually recognized and cherished and yet remain part of a whole.

When we change our thinking we can truly experience a oneness with all things. We then become one with man, nature and the Creative essence. In order to get to this point we will have to shake off the old structure: belief systems that do not allow oneness to be present. It will be like transplanting a rare flower. First you remove the old soil and then carefully put the flower in a new pot that has good

soil to support its growth. Then we water the flower with love and can experience
such a beautiful, sustaining fragrance. The seeds of that flower will create new
flowers and peace will prevail in our world. It will happen because we have
tended to our own gardens and celebrated the garden of mankind together.

Perhaps this is the spiritual task for Reiki at this time. With the use of Reiki we
return to our spiritual nature, we touch our souls, experience our light and then
are able to see and experience others' light and love. Nothing has changed about
the message of Reiki in all these years. I believe what is changing is that more
people are learning Reiki, using Reiki and becoming more in touch with their
spiritual nature. Reiki is now all around the world, so that the potential is greater
for unconditional love to have an effect. Also, we as people have lived so much of
our lives in disharmony and are finally able to understand that we can create
something different.

To me it seems we are in an age of spiritual renaissance. It is refreshing to see
religious and spiritual leaders coming together, seeking communication and unity.
Men and women acknowledge the importance of the individual and work
together for a peaceful resolution and return to our spiritual nature. This is
happening all over the world now. It is certainly happening in the country in
which I live, the Czech Republic, and the Dalai Lama has recently made an
appearance here. What an important time we live in, what opportunities await us.
All we must do, can choose to do, is say, Yes!

I believe that in this time we are in the process of building a bridge to all humanity. In a country where there are such beautiful old bridges, we have an opportunity to start the bridging process ourselves, together. Just as within ourselves our
hearts bridge our spiritual energy to our physical, it is time to build bridges with
our hearts to each other. Reaching out to others with compassion, understanding
and a willingness to create something new and exciting.

In my normal meditative practice I use the symbolism of the bridge, a bridge of
light that all can use to cross back and forth. I like to think of my bridge
resembling the Charles Bridge in Prague. It is not too narrow, nor too high, it
affords people an opportunity to see beauty as they cross and have space to stop
for a while and not block the traffic. I also enjoy the celebration of day-to-day life.
It is active and full of life. It has a history and has supported many people's jour-
neys. I believe that it is important to use our imaginations and visions in creating
what we wish for. To have a picture of something: perfect end results that we can
move towards. Of course space must be there for the creative essence to help in
the process. Involving all our senses in the creation of our dreams and desires is
all part of who we are and are becoming.

If we do not use all of ourselves in the process of creation, which part will get left
out? That is why it is so important to be in harmony. When our minds say one
thing and our hearts another, all we end up with is disharmony, and because a
reactive mind is so strong it will usually win over the heart. That is why we are
where we are now. Mankind's hearts have been closed and the reactive mind has

been driving us down this separate road. Along this road is a world of winners and losers, dog eat dog, the strongest survive, the richest prevail. All this is ego-generated and mind-powered. Only when the heart leads in combination with a mind that is responsible can we create the bridges needed to each other.

Looking back over my life I can see times where there was such an inner struggle a war of sorts was being fought within me. Also in my life at that time I was in discord with the people around me. My friends all seemed be struggling with their own personal wars and together we held corporate beliefs about the world and how we must be to survive.

It is a bit like experiencing our teenagers reaching that time when they need to declare their independence. They want to be different from the family, to be individual, and yet band together in disharmony. They feel misunderstood; parents are foreign and usually represent an authority to struggle against. Ah, the process of awakening hormones throws us into disarray.

We can return to harmony. However, if we have adopted prejudiced belief systems, the war continues. Our prejudice includes ideas about ourselves. Sometimes it seems easier to love others than to love ourselves.

To me it seems that we are born in spiritual innocence and purity only to travel away from it as we grow up. Our reactions create belief systems that are false, yet we defend them against all odds. At some point there is a return to that spiritual

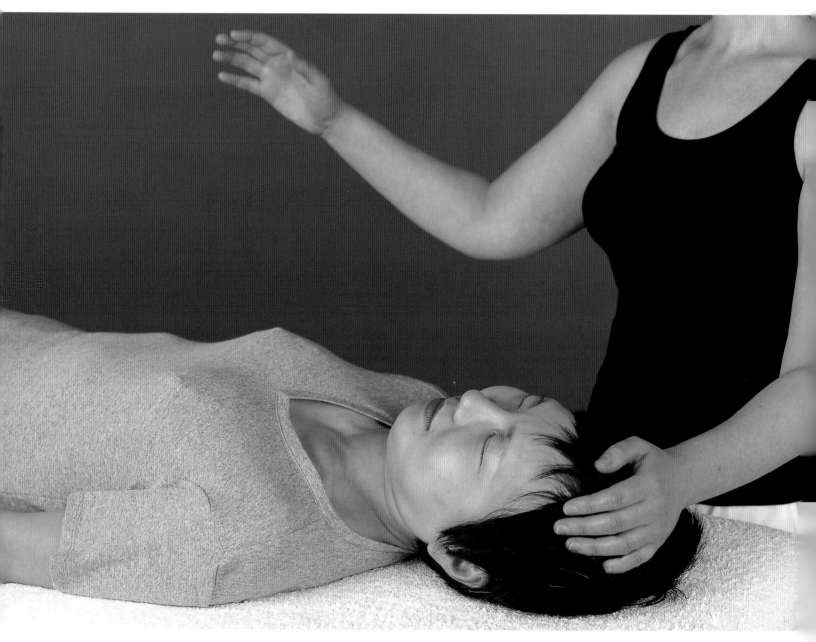

essence. This happens in an awakening moment: perhaps we experience tragedy, illness, or are touched by a moment of profound truth. We may experience this in church or on top of a mountain or even in an initiation process for Reiki. Once we re-experience this spark of divine wisdom, our spiritual innocence and purity, it is held before us like a beacon of light to return to. We are called home to the light.

When I have been asked if this is the message of Reiki, I can only say it is the message as I experience it. All Masters of Reiki are different, all teach from a different perspective, we all have had different life experiences. We certainly are all in our own process of becoming more real and truthful, being mastered by Reiki. It is very important to learn to be discerning when choosing someone to study with or, for that matter, even a book to read. For certain we are all drawn to a person for some reason. There comes a moment where we are given the opportunity to redefine ourselves.

## CHOOSING A MASTER OF REIKI

The title Master of Reiki has lost some of its original meaning as more new Reiki systems are introduced, and courses have been introduced that can make a person a Master in a weekend. So the very title Master can no longer be relied on to distinguish someone who has taken time to come into the work and represents the 'form' at its finest.

How does a person who wishes to take a Reiki seminar find a Master to study with?

You will find courses advertised in various publications, some will have the price and location or the type of course. So if you were shopping for price, you might think that you should go for the course that is the least expensive: 'after all, who are they to charge so much for something so good?' Or perhaps you are looking for a course in a particular town, as it would be more convenient.

You also have to decide which school of Reiki to choose. There is Usui Reiki, XZY Reiki: how do you know which is the best? Then there are all those Masters of Reiki, but what do you know about them and how long they have been teaching? Who can you ask about these questions? What are the important criteria in making this choice?

Part of the problem is that we are not taught to be discerning, so we just take what is available. We do exactly that when we read a book. We assume that the author has more knowledge than we do. I write books out of my own personal experience. If you find what you read helpful and can embrace it, then do so. But it is important that you use your power of discernment. If you read something that you do not agree with, that is fine, I am only offering you a point of view. We are all individuals and have the power of choice.

In order to exercise our power of choice wisely, we must find out what the different options are. To find out what the differences are we must ask questions. The best people to ask are the Masters themselves and people who have taken their courses.

One of the most important things I look for when I choose to work or take a course with someone is who they are within themselves. In other words, what are their levels of personal and spiritual integrity, and their level of consciousness? Also, what is the level of congruency within their personal, professional and spiritual lives. Do they, as much as possible, 'walk the walk' or is it mostly just talk?

Reiki is a spiritual system. A system that many believe is based on unconditional love. If a Master is teaching fear-based philosophy, or denigrating another Master, I do not think this behaviour is 'walking the walk'.

Often, when people feel insecure, they have the tendency to ridicule another person so that the other person seems smaller or less than they do in order to feel better about themselves. Others will use their position as a Master to exercise power over others. They claim to have all the answers so that their students feel dependent upon them. This is a Guru complex.

What is important to me is that the person I study with is one who empowers others. This person chooses to walk beside people while acknowledging the majesty and uniqueness of each individual. These people share their experience and allow space for the individual to have theirs.

Here are some questions that you can ask to help you to use your power of choice. These are only suggestions: if there is something else that you feel is very important to you, by all means ask it.

1   Tell me about yourself and your background.

2   How did you come to Reiki and how has it affected your life?

3   Why did you choose to become a Master?

4   How long did it take you to become a Master of Reiki and what is your lineage?

5   How long have you been teaching Reiki and how many students do you have?

6   Is there some particular reason why you do this work, some personal vision behind this choice?

7   Are you part of a Reiki organization and if so, does the organization have a code of ethics, and what is provided for the student?

8   Have you been involved or are you involved in treating clients in a clinical situation?

9   What types of illness or disharmony have you worked on with Reiki?

10   How do you view your role in a Reiki session?

11   Who does the Reiki, or who is healing?

12   How do you facilitate Reiki or get it?

13   Do you have long-term students?

14   Do you provide support for your students and if so what support is available?

Here are some questions that you can ask students of a particular Master of Reiki.

1  **Did you feel the course lived up to your expectations?**
2  **What was one of the most important experiences for you in the seminar?**
3  **Do you think that you will continue in your Reiki journey with this Master?**
4  **Would you recommend this course to others?**
5  **Are you using the Reiki energy and experiencing results?**
6  **What stands out in your mind about the Master of your course?**
7  **Do you feel empowered in your Reiki?**

One of the most important aspects a Master can bring to their students is the promotion of self-love and joy of living. In that message is also the opportunity to be of service to the people of our world. We can co-create a peace-filled world to live in, starting with ourselves.

## TREATING YOURSELF

Treating yourself with Reiki is so simple. Everywhere you are, Reiki is. Whenever you feel stress or pain, or are feeling generally 'out of sorts', all you need to do is give yourself a treatment by placing your hands on yourself.

The daily use of Reiki brings about an inner balance, so that many illnesses will not be able to develop. Your emotions will be balanced. Your life indeed takes on a

new quality and peace. When you are using Reiki, you are loving yourself and the creative force within you. This loving energy helps you to transform your will and ego to 'Thy-will-be-done'. The use of Reiki in our personal lives offers us a means of balance, so that we attain a healthy mind, body and spirit. Reiki helps you to experience self-love directly and, as a result, you develop a loving relationship with yourself.

## A SUGGESTION FOR DAILY SELF-TREATMENTS

Reiki does not end after you take the seminar. Each person must take on the responsibility of treating themselves. Only you can determine your rate of progress, by the level of commitment you are willing to make. You are your own master and being committed to your own self-healing is the best present you can give yourself.

Lie down or sit comfortably. Start with your head and slowly work down over your whole body, front and back. Include all your chakras, organs, even the soles of your feet. Allow your intuition to guide you to the areas that you feel need energy. This is excellent to do when you first wake up in the morning, or when you are going to bed.

Many people first take a Reiki course in order to bring about a sense of well-being in themselves. Once this is realized, then it is natural to turn it outwards to others.

## TREATING OTHERS

During the first degree course, you will be taught several positions to use in the treatment of other people. These are only suggestions, but they are positions I have found effective. I advise you to allow your hands to go intuitively where they want to during a treatment.

# General Principles for Working with Reiki

## THE SETTING FOR TREATMENT

Reiki works on a busy street, a train, or anywhere. However, I have found it best to have a specific room or area where you work which is harmonious. It is very relaxing for the person who receives the energy, and at the same time helps you to be relaxed and open.

## WORK SPACE AND COMFORT

It is best to have a massage table that is the proper height for you to sit at during treatment. This table will provide comfort both for the person receiving the energy and yourself, as you are both supported. It is important because the treatment may last an hour.

If a massage table is not available, you could use a dining table, with a foam pad on it, or blankets to pad the space where the person will lie. If the person is bed-ridden, position yourself so that you can easily reach them without discomfort. It is less tiring to keep your own back straight than to be bending over or standing for long periods of time. Remember that comfort for both of you is important.

## CLOTHING AND COVERING OF THE RECIPIENT DURING TREATMENT

The person remains clothed during the treatment. If they have tight belts, they can be loosened. Shoes can be removed, as well as any binding outer garments.

During the session, be sure to provide the recipient with adequate cover so that they remain warm. Remember that Reiki radiates heat, and when the hands change location, a cooling can take place. If the room is cool, it could be chilling to the person, so you might cover them with a lightweight blanket, even in the summer months.

## HYGIENE

It is important for you to know that your hands are not magnets for negative energy. They do not collect energy, but rather balance and harmonize everything that they touch. Certainly wash your hands before and after a treatment, where it is possible. If you are treating an open infection, wear protective sterile gloves or place a sterile gauze bandage over the infected area, before putting your hand down. Keep the treatment area in a state of cleanliness and order.

## MUSIC AND BEING CENTRED

Meditative music is very conducive to the relaxation of the recipient and the channel alike. It is most important that you are in a state of harmony. If you are 'centred', then a greater quality of energy can flow through you. Stress = disharmony; relaxation = harmony. If you are in a state of disharmony, work on yourself first. This demonstrates your willingness to apply the principles of Reiki to yourself, and enables you to become balanced and open before you begin working with another person. If you are in a relaxed state, the other person will relax much more readily.

## INVOCATION BEFORE TREATMENT

Although no invocation is required to make Reiki work, if you have a religious philosophy you may wish to say a silent prayer before placing your hands on someone, such as:

'Thank you for allowing me to be an instrument for your divine healing energy. May it go to all people who are willing to receive it.'

## BEFORE THE TREATMENT

Talk with the person, to find out what the physical and/or emotional imbalances might be. Four sessions are usually required to complete the initial energy

balancing. Treat with as many sessions as you both feel are necessary for the healing effect to take place. If it is possible, all four treatments should be given on successive days. This will stimulate the body to cleanse itself of any toxins. I also recommend to people that they drink a lot of water (at least 2 litres every day), to support the natural detoxification process.

## TOUCHING: A PROFESSIONAL ATTITUDE

Many people have difficulty touching or being touched in the private reproductive areas of the body. In most cases it is not necessary to make direct contact, thus eliminating any uneasiness.

## MORE ABOUT TOUCHING

A big difference between some other forms of energy work and Reiki is that we touch the body. With some other forms of energy work, the therapist works in the person's field of energy, or aura. The philosophy is that, if the aura is in a state of harmony, then the physical body will follow. This is true. When we are touching the physical body, the energy is also going into the aura, so that it can become balanced. When you place your hands on someone, they know that you care about them and that you are there for them in that present moment. I believe that we do not touch each other enough. We touch our children, but at some mysterious time, we stop touching them. They are 'too old for a cuddle'. I see various ages and sizes of people, all of whom have an inner child in them who is

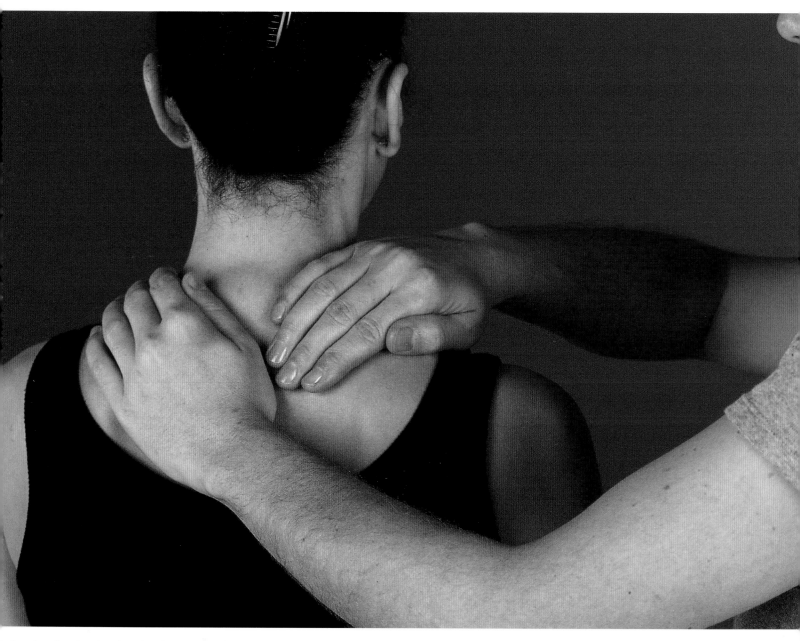

saying, 'please hug me and love me'. We do not usually ask for a hug, because we are afraid of rejection. Reiki is a way of loving and being loved. We can reach out and touch that inner child, which is in all of us, with unconditional love.

## TALKING DURING THE TREATMENT

Quiet conversation can be helpful, especially if the recipient feels like opening up and discussing the emotions surrounding their state of unwellness. However, do not feel it is necessary for them to talk or that you must investigate to find the cause, if the person does not want to share this information. Sometimes, emotional discussions can be inhibiting to the healing process, causing unnecessary tension, pain and remorse. Since Reiki works on all levels of the body, mind and spirit, it is not necessary for you to counsel. By providing Reiki to take away physical pain, the person will, in their own time, go inward and begin to gain awareness of the emotional factors that may well be the cause or the result of this particular unwellness.

Distracting noise, such as children playing or the television being on, is not conducive to healing. If you must be interrupted to have a conversation, it is suggested that you leave the healing setting. Use discretion.

## HAND PRESSURE AND THE NEEDS OF THE RECIPIENT

Place your hands on the body using relaxed and gentle touch. Any pressure or heaviness from your hands may be uncomfortable to the recipient. To ensure that your hands are relaxed, you must be comfortable. Reposition yourself if you are straining from the position you are in. If you are uncomfortable, you will think more about your discomfort than the needs of the recipient. The healing setting must include your comfort, except in an emergency, when the other person's needs outweigh your own.

It is important to consider the needs of the recipient. There are many variables, due to the differences between the individuals you will treat. The following questions should be asked of all clients:

1   Is the room temperature too warm or too cold? The temperature should
    be comfortable.
2   Does the client need a pillow under their head, for comfort?
3   Does the client need a pillow under their knees? This can help to reduce
    the pressure on the lower back, which is especially helpful for people who
    have lower back problems, including pregnant women and women with a
    tilted uterus.

You want the recipient to be comfortable at all times in the healing setting. The temperature, lighting, music, and your state of relaxation and harmony all need consideration. Experience will provide you with additional ideas of how best to meet the needs of the recipient. The most important factor is to be loving.

## PERMISSION FOR TREATMENT AND THE EXCHANGE OF ENERGY FOR YOUR TIME (FEE)

Throughout the world, there are different regulations governing the practice of treating people. Obviously, if you are a doctor who is also practising Reiki, you can apply Reiki whenever you want to and feel that it is necessary. The biggest problem is the amount of time you have to spend with a patient in relation to the amount of time necessary for the treatment. Reiki is being used successfully by many different professional groups, such as masseurs, medical assistants, nurses, midwives, drug counsellors, psychotherapists and beauty therapists.

It is very important that you never make a diagnosis, or even use the word 'diagnosis'. Never advise the client to discontinue medication that their doctor has prescribed; nor should you prescribe any medication, unless you are a medical practitioner. Never undertake any action which will invade beneath the skin's surface.

Some people who are doing Reiki as a profession call it a relaxation technique and are able to do this as the person is indeed relaxed. As the client remains dressed, you are not coming into direct contact with them.

Legal regulations vary from country to country. I advise you to find out about the legal requirements of your professional organizations before using Reiki as part of your work. It is better not to use the term 'patient', but to use the words 'client' or 'recipient' to describe the people you are treating, so that people do not feel you might be illegally running a medical practice. In all cases where you have any doubt, check the legal situation in your country.

When I was working in Great Britain, I joined the National Federation of Spiritual Healers, as this organization is legally recognized in the UK. Doctors even refer people to members of this organization for treatment.

With regard to payment, people are not paying you (exchanging energy) for the Reiki energy, but rather for your time. You have a worth or value. Giving and receiving should be in balance. There needs to be an exchange either of services, or of money, for this time. Often, when we work with someone in the family, there is a natural exchange taking place, where people are doing things for each other. Reiki practitioners do establish a fee when they offer their time to channel this energy on a professional basis. The fee sets a value on the service: wellness has a value, and ultimately reflects the feeling of worthiness and self-love of the person seeking to change their health.

The person must ask for treatment – this is a spiritual law. By asking, they open themselves to receive and have expressed a conscious decision to be involved in the process. The recipient is the healer. The channel is only an instrument

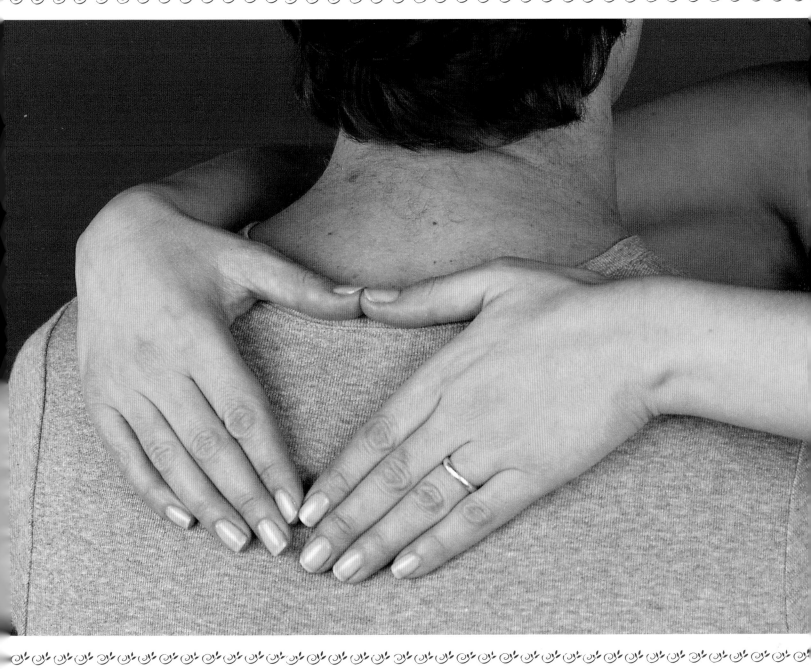

through which the energy flows. If you do not receive permission, or are not asked, and work on someone anyway, you are exerting your will, your ego, on them. This is not Reiki.

## SENSITIVITY TO THE RECIPIENT'S PAIN

It is not uncommon to be sensitive to the recipient's pain. Normally, you feel the pain in the same area of your body as the person who is receiving the energy. This does not mean that you are taking on their pain or energy and will keep it. The level of feeling is merely a barometer, telling you how much energy the recipient will need to balance the area where the pain is located.

Reiki is *not* a system of taking on or extracting pain from someone. If you are left with pain once the session is complete, then you have, at some level, desired (consciously or unconsciously) to retain the person's pain. This usually occurs when you have the thought 'I want to make you well', or 'I will heal you and take away your pain'.

In many instances, I find people develop more sensitivity to feeling, the more they use Reiki. You begin to have a sensitivity to the environment, as well as personal energies. When this sensitivity is developed, it leads to the perception level called 'clairsentience' or clear feeling. Clarity comes when a person clearly distinguishes the origin of the energy, and controls the influence it projects.

Learning to know the difference between your feelings, pains and energy balance, from those of another person, takes training. It is best to ask yourself objectively: 'Is this my own emotion, or pain?' Always be aware of how your own body feels before placing your hands on someone else.

Once you have been reawakened by a Reiki Master, when you place your hands on yourself or another person in order to transfer the energy, you may start to feel warmth and/or a tingling sensation. Leave your hands there as long as these sensations remain as intense. Once the feeling starts to dissipate, move your hands to another area. The energy comes through the palms and fingertips of your hands. The proper amount of Reiki has been given to the recipient when the sensation in your hands subsides.

## DURATION AND TIMING OF TREATMENTS

It usually takes about an hour to give a full body treatment. It is always best, if you have the time, to treat the whole body, as you are treating the cause as well as the resulting illness. When you are working on children, it usually takes half of the time, depending on their size. If you are only treating one area of the body, allow 20 to 30 minutes; with children, of course, the time needed will be less.

Healing is a wondrous process. All of us have our own rhythm and time for things. No two people are alike and, because of that uniqueness, the healing experience is different almost every time. I find that if I have an expectation of

how someone should respond to treatment, I am not being sufficiently open to their healing process. It may appear that one person has immediate relief from their symptoms, while others may experience an aggravation of their symptoms, or the pain may become more intense. In this case it can indicate that the healing is taking place on a deeper level; on a physical level, the acceleration of the healing process can cause an increase in the intensity of the symptoms, which seems quickly to dissipate, usually by the third day. This is referred to as a 'healing crisis'. In such cases more Reiki should be given.

Daily application of Reiki to yourself and others for 20–30 minutes will help to keep your system balanced, and will act as a preventive against illness and stress.

In the following pages, the specific imbalances are mentioned not for the purposes of diagnosis, but for your education only. Always trust your intuition when working with Reiki; respond to that inner voice.

## SCANNING THE BODY

1  Relax and centre yourself. Take a few deep, relaxing breaths. Stretch your fingers and your arms. Loosen your shoulders.
2  Sensitize your hands by rubbing them together for a few seconds. Stop, then take another breath so that you are not just feeling the heat that you have just generated by friction.

3    Begin to feel the energy between your own hands, before you try to feel the energy of someone else.

4    Imagine where the edge of the person's aura is, then use your hands as an extension of your mind. It is important to scan for what is there, not what your mind might think is there. This is not a mental exercise, but a feeling one. Start at the head and move your hands down one side of the body, keeping them in the aura, just above the body's surface.

5    When you reach the feet move up the other side of the body, back towards the head. (It does not matter which side, left or right, you start with, as long as the whole of the body is covered.) Make your movements graceful and keep your fingers moving as they follow the contours of the aura.

6    Make sure that you continue to breathe normally. If you hold your breath, it will keep you from feeling anything.

7    Keep your spine straight, or at least return often to a straight back position, so that you do not lose the nerve impulses and lessen your ability to feel.

8    Notice areas of the body that are cold or extremely hot. These are areas of imbalance and will need Reiki.

9    Trust your intuition: the more you practise feeling the energy with your hands, the more sensitive you will become.

The following diagrams are for your information. Consider them as a map to help you find a specific part of the body. They are not intended to be used for diagnosis. Remember, Reiki directs itself to the area where it is needed.

*Trunk of Body with Major Organs – Front View*

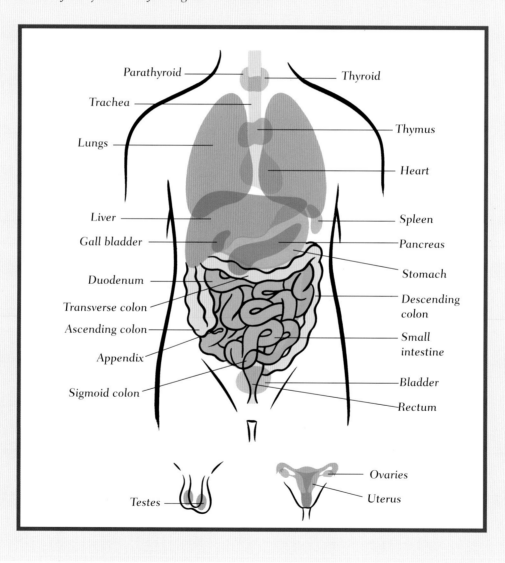

*Trunk of Body with Major Organs – Back View*

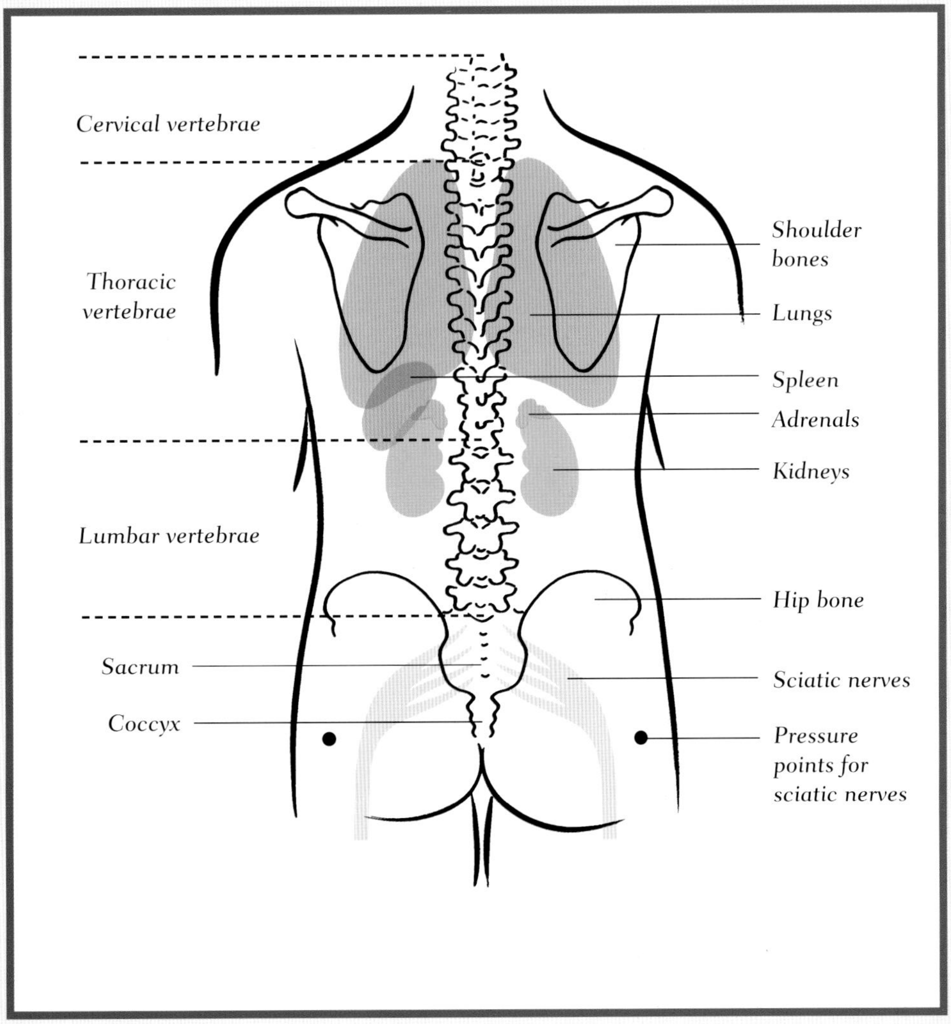

Cervical vertebrae

Thoracic vertebrae

Shoulder bones

Lungs

Spleen

Adrenals

Kidneys

Lumbar vertebrae

Hip bone

Sacrum

Sciatic nerves

Coccyx

Pressure points for sciatic nerves

# Self-
# treatment
# Positions

# Front of the Head

## POSITION 1

The hands cover the front of the face, with the tips of the fingers touching the forehead. The hands are together, giving yourself space to breathe.

*Specific imbalances being treated:* sinus blockage; headaches; migraines; strokes; allergies; upper respiratory congestion; hay fever; gum problems; toothache.

*Chakra: Third eye* *Glands: Pituitary, thalamus*

## POSITION 2

The tips of the fingers are placed at the midline of the crown of the head. The hands rest gently on the sides of the head.

*Specific imbalances and functions being treated:*
mental organization; head injuries; strokes; stress; the left and right hemispheres of the brain; motor and thinking functions; headaches and migraines.

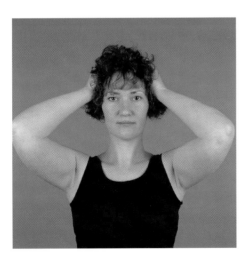

***Chakra:*** *Crown* **Glands:** *Pineal, hypothalamus*

## THROAT

One hand is placed on the throat and the other rests on the chest, directly below the first.

*Specific imbalances and functions being treated:* energy stimulation; stress; immune system stimulation for better absorption of calcium; nervousness; metabolism problems.

*Chakra: Throat **Glands:** Thyroid, parathyroid, thymus*

# Back of the Head

## POSITION I

The heels of the hands are cupped at the lower portion of the skull, where the head ends and the neck begins. The fingers extend upward, with the thumbs and index fingers touching.

*Specific imbalances being treated:* headaches and migraines; strokes; eye problems; head injuries; nosebleeds (use with an ice pack applied to the base of the neck).

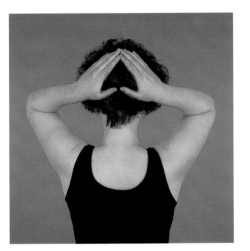

**Chakra:** *Third eye* **Gland:** *Pineal*

## POSITION 1 (ALTERNATIVE)

**This position may be more comfortable. Place hands horizontally behind the head. One hand is on the occipital ridge, the other is below.**

*Specific imbalances being treated:* headaches and migraines; strokes; eye problems; head injuries; nosebleeds (use with an ice pack applied to the base of the neck).

***Chakra:*** *Third eye* ***Gland:*** *Pineal*

# Front of the Body

## POSITION 1 (BREAST)

Cup the breast, one hand resting on the top of the breast and the other holding the lower part of the breast, so that the entire breast is covered.

Note: Men also have breasts and will need treatment in this area.

*Chakra: Crown Glands: Pineal, hypothalamus*

## POSITION 1 (ALTERNATIVE)

One hand is placed on each
breast, the right hand on the right
breast and the left hand on the
left breast.

*Specific imbalances and functions
being treated:*
cysts or tumours in the breast;
lymphatic disorders; milk production
in nursing mothers.

***Chakra:*** *Heart* ***Glands:*** *Thymus*

## POSITION 2

Hands are placed under the breast line, with the middle fingertips touching. Hands are placed gently on the body. The fingertips meet at the centreline of the body.

*Specific area and imbalances being treated:*

lymphatic disorders; lungs.

*Chakra: Solar plexus*

## POSITION 3

Moving your hands down one hand width from Position 2, you should be close to the waistline. Your fingertips are touching and meeting at the centreline of the body.

*Specific areas and imbalances being treated:*

**Right side of the body:** gall bladder; gallstones; upper colon; colitis; constipation; mucus accumulation.

**Left side of the body:** upper colon; stomach; ulcers; spasms; digestive problems; pancreas; diabetes; blood sugar imbalance; haemophilia.

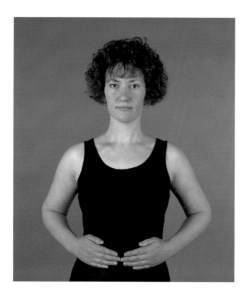

*Chakra: Solar plexus Glands: Adrenals*

## POSITION 4

**Moving your hands down one hand width from Position 3, you should be below the waist, your fingertips touching at the midline of the body.**

*Specific areas and imbalances being treated:*
lower colon; lower digestive disorders; small intestine; spasms.

***Chakras:*** *Sacral and solar plexus* ***Glands:*** *Adrenals*

## POSITION 5

**Your hands point downwards, with the thumbs and index fingers touching. The fingertips touch the pubic bone.**

*Specific imbalances being treated:* female and male reproductive disorders; pain during menstruation; bladder and urinary tract infections; arthritis.

Note: When there is a migraine headache it can be a sign of sexual stress. This position and all three head positions should be used.

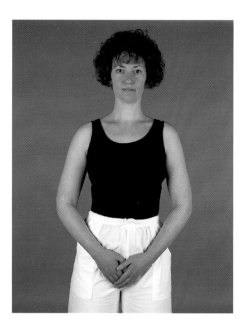

***Chakras:*** *Root and sacral* **Glands:** *Testes, ovaries and adrenals*

# Back of the Body

## POSITION I

**Reach up and place the hands on the shoulder muscles. Touch the middle fingers together at the centre of the spine.**

*Specific imbalances being treated:* tension; throat problems; spinal problems; headaches from neck tension.

*Chakra: Throat **Glands:** Thyroid and parathyroid*

## POSITION 2

These are two separate moves, not to be done at the same time.

A  Take your left hand and reach up, placing it on the left shoulder blade.

B  With your right hand reach up and place it on the right shoulder blade.

*Specific imbalances being treated*: nervousness; tension in the upper back; lung and spinal problems.

*Chakra: Heart Gland: Thymus*

## POSITION 3

**Place your hands one hand width above the waist line with middle fingers touching.**

*Specific imbalances and areas being treated:*
diabetes; hypoglycaemia; hyperglycaemia; stress; migraines; kidneys; high blood pressure; infections; adrenal glands; arthritis.

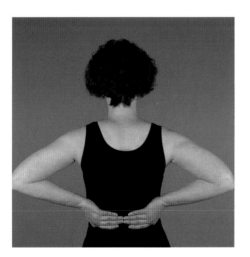

***Chakra:*** *Solar plexus* ***Glands:*** *Adrenals*

## POSITION 3 (ALTERNATIVE)

**Place one hand on top of the other over the centre of the spine, at the level of the waist.**

*Specific imbalances and areas being treated:*

diabetes; hypoglycaemia;

hyperglycaemia; stress; migraines;

kidneys; high blood pressure;

infections; adrenal glands; arthritis.

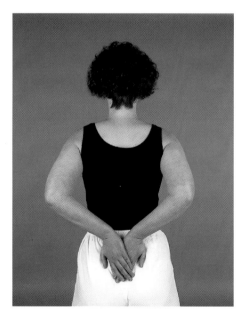

***Chakra:** Solar plexus **Glands:** Adrenals*

## POSITION 4

The hands point downward, with the heels of your hands at the waistline and the middle fingers touching the top of the tail bone.

*Specific imbalances being treated:* intestinal disorders; reproductive disorders; lower back problems.

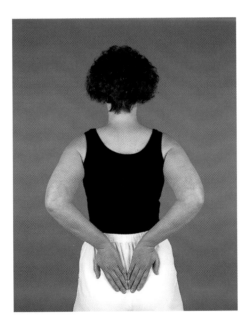

*Chakra: Sacral and root* **Glands:** *Testes or ovaries, and adrenals*

# Treating
# Others

# The Best Approach
# when Working with Someone Else

It is generally best to start at the head, so that the person relaxes. Move around the body, maintaining contact with the person as you change position. When you are finished with the front ask the person to turn over, so that you can work on the back. Again, move around the whole body, so that the entire back, back of the head and back of the legs are treated.

It may be more comfortable for the person to have a pillow under the head when they are lying on their back, as well as a pillow under the knees. When the person turns over onto their stomach, move the pillow under the chest area, so that they can breathe, and the other pillow under their ankles.

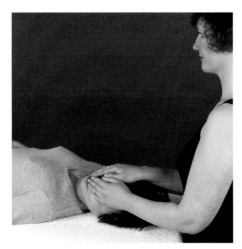
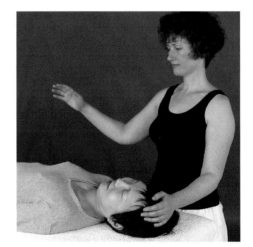

If the person has a problem lying on their stomach, if they are pregnant for example, they can lie on one side so that you can treat the back area. Put a pillow between the recipient's thighs in this position to increase their comfort.

Selected positions for the treatment of others are given below. It is best if the person can lie down.

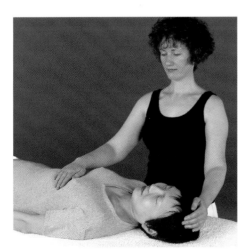 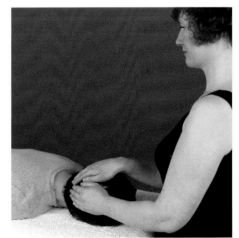

# Front of the Head

## POSITION 1

You will be sitting or standing at the head of the person, with the heels of the hands placed on the forehead, index fingers and thumbs adjoining. Gently rest your hands on the person's face, allowing them to breathe easily.

You may put a tissue over the eyes if you wish, but do not cover the nose.

*Specific imbalances being treated:* eye problems; sinus blockage; headaches; migraines; strokes; allergies; upper respiratory congestion; hay fever; gum problems; toothache.

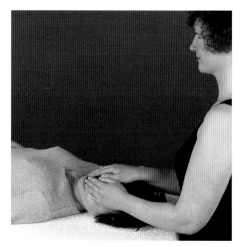

***Chakra:*** *Third eye* ***Glands:*** *Pituitary, thalamus*

## POSITION 2

**Sitting or standing at the head of the person, place the heels of the hand at the centreline of the crown, your hands extending down the sides of the head towards the ears (as if you are cupping the head in your hands).**

*Specific imbalances and functions being treated:*
mental organization; head injuries; stroke; stress; the right and left hemispheres of the brain; motor and thinking functions; headaches; migraines.

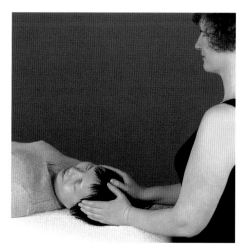

*Chakra: Crown Glands: Pineal, hypothalamus*

# Front of the Body

## POSITION I

Sitting or standing at the head of the person, bring your hands slightly below the neckline, your index fingers and thumbs adjoining, and rest your hands on the upper chest region.

*Specific imbalances and functions being treated:* energy stimulation; stress; immune system stimulation; weight control; calcium absorption; nervousness; metabolism.

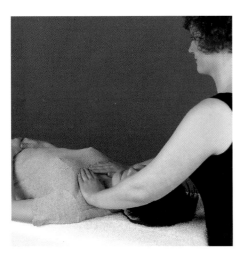

*Chakra: Throat Glands: Thyroid, parathyroid, thymus*

## POSITION 1 (ALTERNATIVE)

Sitting or standing at the side of the person, put the hand that is the closest to the person on the upper chest region pointing downward towards the lower body. Place the other hand pointing upward on the other side: you will have one hand pointing down and the other pointing up, and it will look as if you are making a semi-circle of energy in the region of the throat and upper chest.

*Specific imbalances and functions being treated:*
energy stimulation; stress; immune system stimulation; weight control; calcium absorption; nervousness; metabolism.

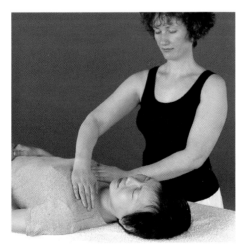

*Chakra: Throat **Glands:** Thyroid, parathyroid, thymus*

## POSITION 2 (BREAST)

Treat the breast as needed. Place one hand on one breast and the other hand on the other breast, or you may cup each breast with both hands in turn. If the person does not want their breasts touched, you can work in the aura just above the breast.

*Specific imbalances being treated:* cysts; tumours; lymphatic disorders; breast pain during menstruation; migraine headaches where sexual tension is indicated.

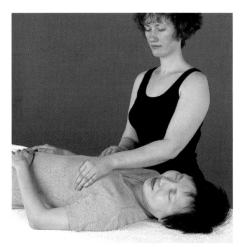

*Chakra: Heart* **Gland:** *Thymus*

## POSITION 3

With hands one hand width lower than the breast, one hand is placed under the breastline on the right side and the other hand is placed on the left side, so that the fingers of one hand touch the heel of the other hand. Rest your hands on the body gently.

*Specific areas and imbalances being treated:*

**Right side of the body:** lower lungs; liver disorders; infections; blood sugar imbalances; digestive problems.

**Left side of the body:** lower lungs; immune system stimulation; spleen; gas release from the heart region.

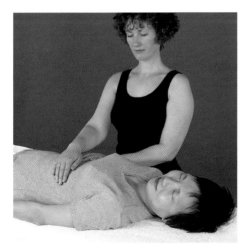

***Chakra:*** *Heart* ***Glands:*** *Thymus, adrenals*

## POSITION 4

Move your hands down one hand width from Position 3. Your hands will be slightly above the waist, the fingertips of one hand touching the heel of the other.

*Specific areas and imbalances being treated:*

**Right side of the body:** gall bladder; gallstones; upper colon; colitis; constipation; mucus accumulation.

**Left side of the body:** upper colon; stomach; ulcers; spasms; digestive problems; pancreas; diabetes; blood sugar imbalance; haemophilia.

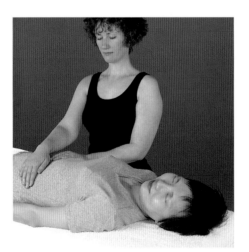

*Chakra: Solar plexus* **Glands:** *Adrenals*

## POSITION 5

**Move your hands down one hand width from position 3. Your hands will be below the waist, the fingertips of one hand touching the heel of the other.**

*Specific functions and imbalances being treated:*
colon and upper small intestine; colitis; digestion; constipation; diverticulitis; stress (solar plexus); mucus accumulation; assimilation of nutrients from food.

***Chakras:*** *Solar plexus and sacral* ***Glands:*** *Adrenals*

## POSITION 6

**One hand is pointing down, resting on the pubic bone to one side. The other hand is pointing up, with the heel of the hand resting on the pubic bone on the other side.**

*Specific areas and imbalances being treated:*
lower intestines; colon; bladder infections; arthritis; cystitis; vagina and uterus; menstrual problems; ovaries; fallopian tubes; migraine headaches where sexual stress is indicated; male reproductive problems.

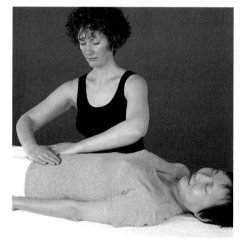

Note: making contact with the reproductive areas of the body is not necessary if a person is uncomfortable with being touched there. Have your hands just above the area, in the aura: you can rest your arms to support your hands, so that they do not become tired.

**Chakras:** *Root and sacral* **Glands:** *Testes, ovaries and adrenals*

# Back of the Head

The person lies on their front, with you sitting at the top of their head. The fingertips touch the lower edge of the skull, where the head ends and the neck begins (the occipital ridge). The hands are joined and placed on the back of the head.

*Specific imbalances being treated:* headaches; stroke; eye problems; migraines; head injuries; nosebleeds (use an ice pack placed at the back of the neck).

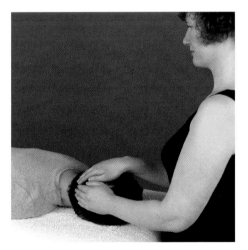

***Chakra:*** *Third eye* ***Gland:*** *Pineal*

# Back of the Body

## POSITION I

Place the heel of one hand on the shoulder muscle, with the middle fingertip touching the channel of the spine (see photo below). The other hand is placed with the fingertips on the shoulder muscle, and the heel of the hand touching the channel of the spine (one hand is up and the other is down).

*Specific imbalances being treated:* tension; throat problems; spinal problems; headaches from neck tension.

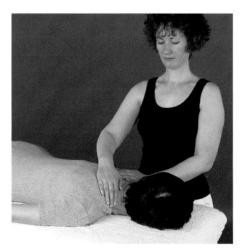

*Chakra:* Throat **Glands:** *Thyroid and parathyroid*

## POSITION 2

Moving your hands down one hand width, one of your hands is on the left shoulder blade, the other is on the right shoulder blade and the heel of one hand is touching the fingertips of the other.

*Specific areas and imbalances being treated:*
nervousness; tension; back of lungs; spinal problems.

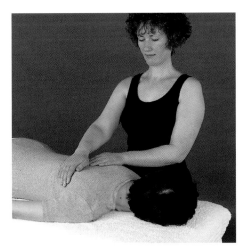

*Chakra: Heart Gland: Thymus*

## POSITION 3

**Move your hands down one hand width from position 2. The heel of your hand is touching the fingertips of the other hand, slightly above the waist. Your hands will be on the adrenal glands and upper portion of the kidney.**

*Specific imbalances being treated:* diabetes; hypoglycaemia; hyperglycaemia; stress; migraines; infections; spinal problems.

Basically, all body imbalances will require additional treatment time on the adrenal glands. Treating the adrenal glands prevents the person from going into shock, or you can treat the adrenals if they are already in shock.

*Chakra: Solar plexus Glands: Adrenals*

## POSITION 4

Move your hands down one hand width. You will be slightly below the waist with the heel of one hand touching the fingertips of the other.

*Specific imbalances being treated:*
kidney problems; arthritis; oedema; high blood pressure; infections.

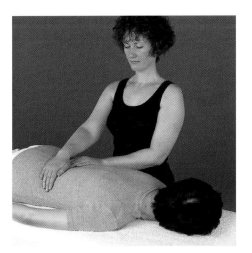

***Chakras:*** *Solar plexus and sacral* ***Glands:*** *Adrenals*

## POSITION 5

One hand is pointing down to the tail-bone and resting on one side of the lower back, to the side of the spine. The other hand is pointing up from the tail-bone on the other side of the lower back, to the other side of the spine.

*Specific imbalances being treated:* intestinal disorders; lower back problems in the lumbar and sacral areas.

*Chakras:* Sacral and root *Glands:* Testes or ovaries and adrenals

# POSITION 5 (ALTERNATIVE)

**Place one hand horizontally across the lower back. The other hand is placed below it, resting on the spine, across the lower back.**

The specific imbalances, chakras and glands being treated are the same as in Position 5.

*Feeling the Energy in Your Hands*

Once you have been using Reiki for a while you may notice an increase in the sensitivity of your hands. You may start to feel the energy move through the part of the body that you are touching. If the area is out of balance you will not feel this at the same time in both hands – it will be erratic. If the area is in balance then the energy will be felt at the same time in both hands –it is synchronized.

In the following special positions for specific illnesses, I usually wait until I have that feeling of being balanced or synchronized, before I move my hands. I am feeling the energy move, as well as the temperature and/or tingling.

Special

Positions

for

Specific

Imbalances

# Earaches, Hearing Loss & Deafness

Place the middle finger gently on the ear opening. The middle finger will be bent to accomplish this. The index finger is placed on the head in front of the ear, while the ring and little finger are placed behind the ear on the head.

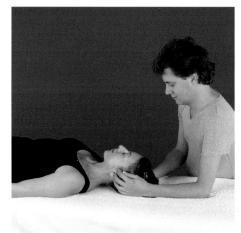

Remember to treat under the jaw for
earaches, as the Eustachian tubes fill
up with pus, fluid and mucus.

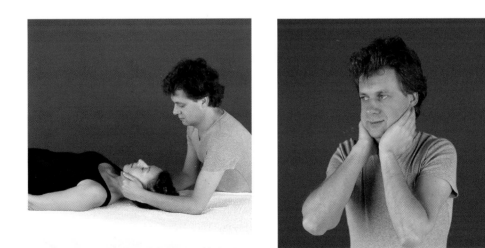

# High or Low Blood Pressure, Strokes & Migraines

**Place one hand on the back of the head on one side. The other hand is placed on the neck on the opposite side, over the carotid artery. Treat until the energy flow is balanced and then place the hands in the reverse positions.**

Note: In cases of very high blood pressure, begin with the hand on the neck for five to ten seconds. Increase the amount of time each session. This will prevent a radical change in blood pressure. Often these problems are a result of other imbalances. It is best to do a full body treatment.

# Immune System Stimulation

Place one hand on the thymus gland (medical doctors say this gland is non-functioning). It is a spiritual centre and does take energy. Then place the other hand on the spleen, which is on the left side of your body.

You are balancing the third and fourth chakras together.

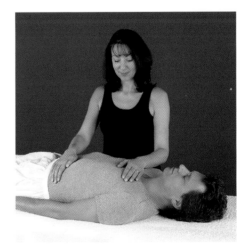

# Poor Circulation in the Legs, Varicose Veins & Lower Lymphatic Disorders

Treat the right and left leg alternately. Place one hand at the top of the leg, inside the thigh. The other hand is placed on the groin and the hands touch where the leg and body are joined together.

Alternate legs as they become balanced.

# Circulation in the Arms
# & Lymphatic Disorders

**If you are treating yourself, you place one hand under the arm in the armpit, alternating to the other side as you feel the energy becoming balanced. If you are working with someone else, place your hands under the arm in the armpit, using both hands.**

This is an excellent position for the treatment of lymphatic disorders, and is a wonderful treatment for toxic build-up in the body. It can also be used for removing cysts in the armpit.

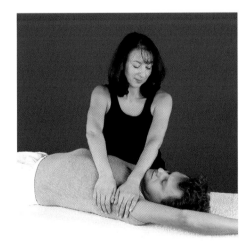

# Lung & Related
# Respiratory Dysfunctions

1   Put one hand down and one
    hand up on the other's upper
    chest, as in Position 1
    (Alternative) on the front
    of the body (see page 79).

2   The hands are placed on the
    breastline, as in Position 2 on
    the front of the body (see page
    80). Move your hands down one
    hand width at a time, leaving
    your hands in place until there
    is a dissipation of the energy,
    and/or you feel the area has

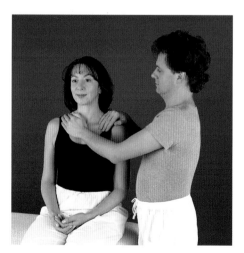
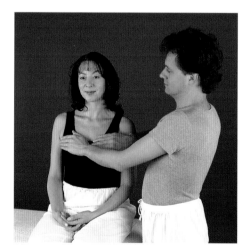

come into balance. Work over the entire lung area; also treat the sides of the body so that you energize the sides of the lungs. It is easier to treat the side of the body if the person is lying on their side.

3   Pay attention to the direction in which your hands are pointing, as you will need to make a circle with the energy. It does not matter which way the circle goes. If I started on the right side of the front of the body, I would work on the back from the left side.

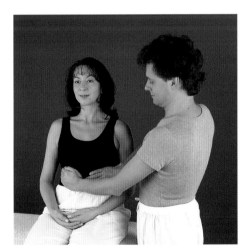

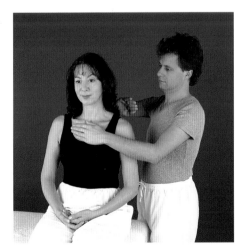

4 On the back of the person, one hand goes up, and the other down, as in Position 1 on the back of the body (see page 86).

5 Work your way down one hand width at a time, as in Positions 2 and 3 on the back (see pages 87–88), in order to energize the whole lung area.

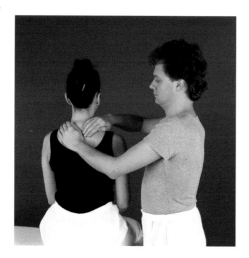

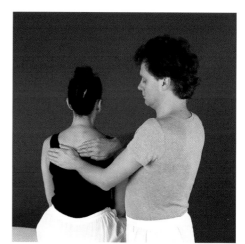

Special note: never place a person
who has pneumonia on their stomach.
You will have to treat their back by
reaching under them, or having them
sit up, if possible. Always lie them at a
30 degree angle, to ensure better
breathing.

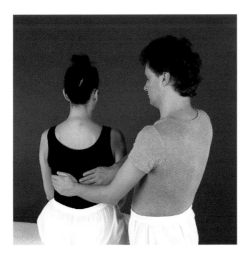

# Prostate Problems in Men & Haemorrhoids in Men & Women

One hand is placed on the lower back in a horizontal position. The other hand is placed over the centre line of the base of the spine, with the fingers pointing down and the middle finger at the very end of the backside.

You will be cupping the rear end with your hand.

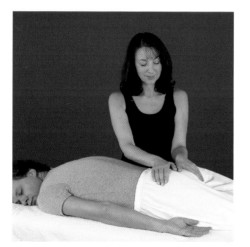

# Prevention of Stress

**To treat yourself, place one hand over the thyroid gland, at the base of the throat. Place the other hand on the solar plexus (the centre of the body above the navel).**

To treat another person, you follow the same directions as the self-treatment. You should wait until there is a dissipation of energy and/or a feeling of balance.

 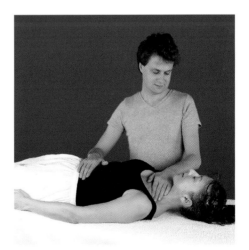

# Heart Imbalance &
# Heart Attacks

1   In all heart imbalance cases
    (except heart attack), you must
    first work under the breast area,
    as in Position 3 on the front of
    the body (see page 81). This
    position enables the person to
    dispel pressure caused by
    accumulated gas.

2   When the gas is expelled, place
    your hands directly over the
    heart in the position shown.

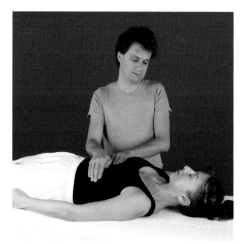

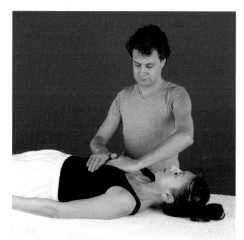

Heart attacks: go directly to the heart. If you know CPR (Cardio-Pulmonary Resuscitation), you would use this technique if the person's heart had stopped beating. If breathing has ceased, then begin resuscitation with one hand on the heart. Reiki has been known to help return a heart to normal operating function after a heart attack.

# Scoliosis (Hardening & Curvature of the & Related Spinal Injuries

1   Place both hands over the trapezius muscles and leave them there until the energy has dissipated.

2   Go down the entire back, using Positions 1, 2, 3 and 4 for treating the back of the body (see pages 86–89). Move down one hand width at a time so that you cover the entire back.

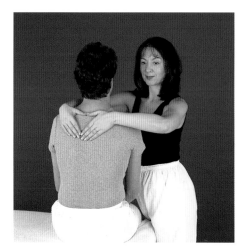

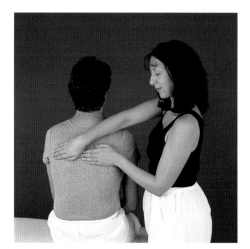

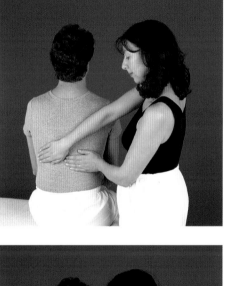

3   Finally, place the hands over the lower back as in Position 5 (Alternative) for the back (see page 91).

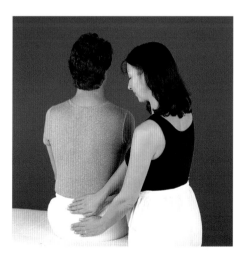

# Sciatica

The following is a neurological diagram of the sciatic nerve, starting at the sacrum and running down the leg. Note the pressure points on the shoulders and also in the buttocks: if they are sore, it is an indication of sciatic problems. Sciatica should be treated using Reiki in conjunction with chiropractic treatment. Ask the person to get a spinal/sacral adjustment first and give them a Reiki treatment immediately afterwards.

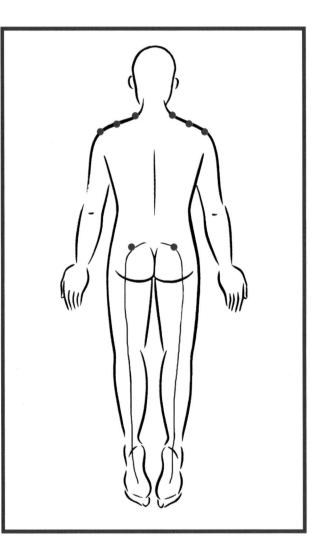

# HOW TO TREAT THE SCIATIC NERVE

1   Working on the back of the
client's body, place one hand
over the sacral bone, with the
fingers of the hand pointing
down to the tip of the tail-bone.
Place the other hand beside it,
with the fingers pointing in the
opposite direction.

2   Move the second hand down the
leg one hand length at a time
until you reach the knee.

3   Beginning at the knee, place the hands on either side of the leg, so that you are sandwiching the leg between your hands. Work your way down, one hand width at a time, until you have worked on the entire lower leg. Finally, place one hand flat on the sole of the foot and the other across the leg, just below the knee.

# Female & Male Reproductive Disorders; Bladder & Urinary Tract Imbalance

**Place one hand over the pubic/uterine area and the other between the legs, with the palm of the hand in front of the reproductive area. (The recipient is to remain clothed during all treatments.)**

*This position can treat the following:*

yeast infection; herpes; vaginitis; cystitis; urinary tract disorders; testicle infection; low sperm count; and bladder disorders.

# First Aid

To prevent shock after an injury or other accident, one hand is placed over the adrenal glands (the glands on top of the kidneys) and the other is placed on the injured area.

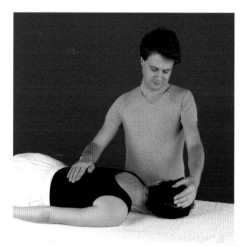

> ### *A Special Note*
>
> ## ACUPRESSURE POINTS
>
> You can use Reiki to activate and balance acupressure points anywhere on the body. To activate the acupressure points for the sinus, place the fingertips of one hand on the upper orbital ridge of the eye socket, then place your index finger of your other hand on the centre of your lower orbital socket. For further information about acupressure points consult your library.

# Sandwiching an Area

You can make a sandwich by placing your hands on either side of an area. The energy comes from both hands, so that the treatment is intensified. You can sandwich a shoulder, hip, elbow, ankle, hand, or the throat, to name but a few areas. If you are working with broken bones, you can treat through the cast. This is an excellent position for treating wounds, broken bones, damaged muscle tissue and burns.

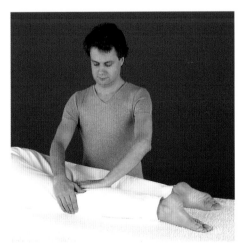

# Running Energy through an Area

**You can run energy through an arm or leg, or through the soles of the feet or the hands. Leave your hands there until you feel the area become synchronized.**

Running energy through soles of the feet harmonizes the whole body.

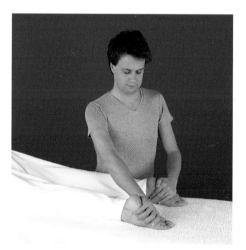

Running energy through the arm can be used to treat the following conditions: arthritis, broken bones, infections, immune system depletion and cancer. Production of white blood cells in the bone marrow is stimulated, which then enter the spleen where they combine with the thymus hormone to produce the 'T'-cell.

Running energy through the leg can be used to treat broken legs and arthritis of the knee, hip or ankle, and to stimulate the immune system.

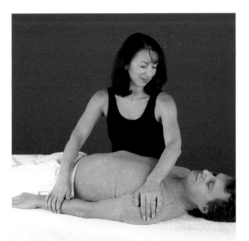

# Raising & Lowering Energy

The following positions should only be done if specifically indicated. To raise the energy in the person's body, or balance their spine, place your left hand on their crown and your right hand at the base of their spine.

To lower the energy in a person, or reduce hypertension and over-sensitivity, place the right hand on the top of the head and the left hand at the base of the spine.

 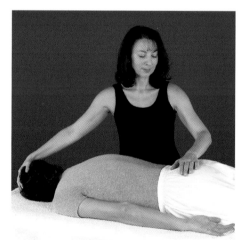

# Releasing Spinal Tension

1   Place the thumb and middle
finger of the right hand on the
occipital ridge at the base of the
skull, and the left hand at the
base of the spine. Wait for the
feeling of being synchronized.

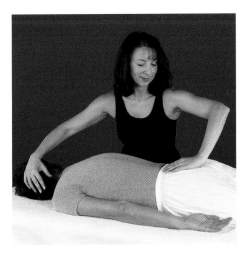

2 Move the hands equally towards the centre of the spine, one hand space at a time. Each move is completed when the pulse is synchronized. The hands never lose contact with the body. Slide your hands towards one another, always touching the spine, moving closer to the area of the greatest tension.

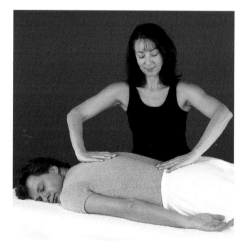 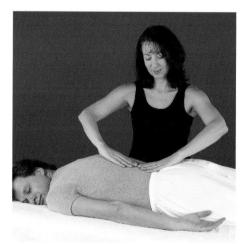

# When You Have
# Finished a Treatment

When you have finished a treatment,
in order to ground the energy and
discontinue transmission, simply put
both hands together.

Other
Ways
of
Using
Reiki

## WORKING WITH A GROUP OF REIKI INSTRUMENTS

When you begin to work together it is important to be synchronized with one another. This need not take a long time, and is usually accomplished by holding hands, taking a few deep, relaxing breaths and finding your own centre. Once this is done, the energy between you should feel even. If there are several of you working on one recipient, each person will Reiki a different part of the body. The treatment time will be much less if there are more people working with a recipient. The greatest compliment is when the recipient is so relaxed that they fall asleep.

## WAYS TO CONNECT WITH EACH OTHER IN A GROUP

When groups of Reiki people come together, we often sit in a circle and put our right hand on the heart of the person on our right; we can also put our left hand over the person whose hand is on our heart. We are feeling the connection of open hearts; the unity and harmony of the entire group. No words are needed: the space is quiet and we are experiencing the never-ending energy of Reiki and our love for one another. We give; we receive; we are one.

Another way to connect is to sit in a long line resting in each other's arms. We are supported, nourished and loved, as we receive from the person behind us and give to the person in front. It is a beautiful, spiritual experience: a time of togeth-erness, not separation. We are unified; we are loved, and it is fun.

## OUR EXPECTATIONS AND PEOPLE'S ATTACHMENT TO ILLNESS

At times, we may expect a particular result when we work on someone else or on ourselves. When that expectation is not fulfilled, we are disappointed. Something else may have taken place, but it was not what we wanted. It is our demand that gets in the way: we must remember that Reiki directs itself, and is perhaps work-ing on a different level from the one we are willing to see. So there may be an internal change, rather than an external one. Do not judge the results of Reiki: it is not your will that will be done. Put your ego aside and be willing to wait for the results to become manifest. Give unconditionally.

Some people are attached to illness on a subconscious level. Even though they say that they want treatment, to give up the illness is a subconscious threat to part of their identity. I have had people come for Reiki treatment with long lists of their diagnoses, starting from the time they were children. 'These are mine', they say. As long as they want to keep them their own on some level, it will be harder to let them go. Reiki Two techniques will help these people to release them. I do encourage people to rid their mind of the concept that they are sick and, rather, to look at the situation as being 'not balanced'. Then we can work together to bring balance about.

*Your mind is a truly powerful tool; it creates your reality in every moment.*
*You are as well as you think you are capable of being.*
MARI

I know you will experience many wonderful results using Reiki. Over the years, I have seen many miracles. I never expect a result; I remain open to what occurs, and I have always been blessed.

## REIKI IN THE TREATMENT OF BABIES AND CHILDREN

Reiki provides the most natural and pleasant way for a mother and father to treat their baby. Parents often hold their baby lovingly anyway, and once one or both of you have learned to give Reiki, you can pass it on to your child every time you stroke or touch it. This energy will intensify the natural relationship that you have with your child. Reiki is a special form of love which all humans thrive on — especially babies.

It is, of course, possible to treat the babies and children of other people, but it is always better for parents to treat their own children, because a loving bond of trust has already been established. I have found that when I treat children, it is best if the child is sleeping, so that he or she is relaxed. I simply sit by their cribs or beds and place my hands on them.

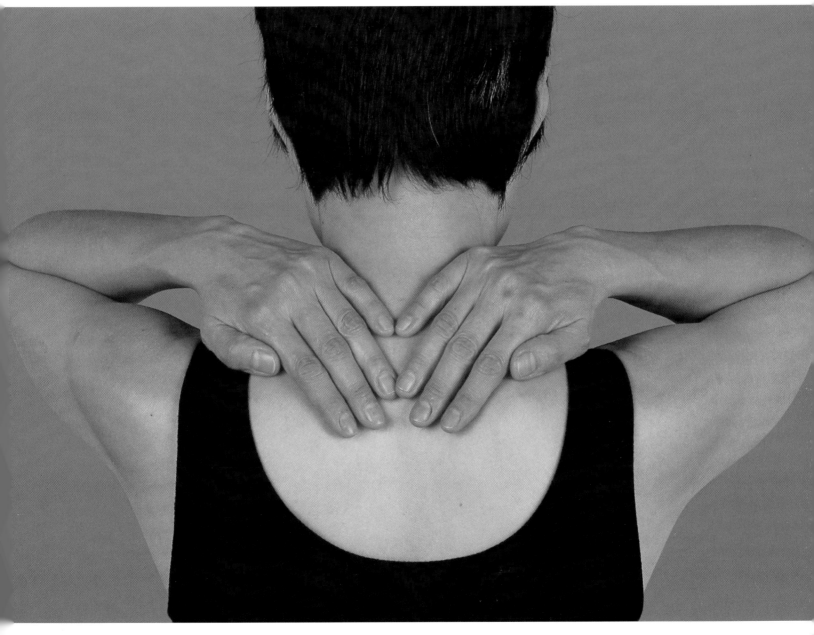

The effects have been quite profound, with some parents finding very relaxed, happy children the next morning and the problems gone or disappearing. It is my recommendation that parents take part in Reiki classes, so that they can treat their own children and support their healing process. This alternative proves to be satisfying in the long run, because it is far less complicated and less expensive.

I have some friends who are students of mine in England. I stay with them when I am travelling in the UK. Sometimes, one of the girls will say, 'Mummy, please give me some Reiki – I can't sleep', or 'Can I have some Reiki? – I don't feel well.' I also find their father sitting by their bed, reading a bedtime story, with one hand on his daughter, giving her Reiki. It has become part of their bedtime routine. I am always filled with gratitude to see how Reiki has become so integrated into their lives. The children love it!

Reiki is also excellent for mothers-to-be. When my daughter, Stacey, was expecting my grandson, Jeremy, I gave her weekly Reiki treatments. It was wonderful. The first time I was with her, she put my hand over her womb and said, 'Here is our baby.' She was relaxed and I felt so connected to my family: to my daughter and to the child growing inside her. I was indeed blessed to be able to love into my grandchild throughout his early development and growth. A mother-to-be can also pass Reiki to her developing baby, influencing the child with that energy for its entire life.

In the Czech Republic there is a hospital for women where all the doctors and nurses give Reiki. In fact meditation music is played in all the labour and delivery

rooms. The noticeable results are that the births are easier, mother and child are calm and filled with love, and the connection of the staff with the new families is warm and sincere. A nice way to start a new life, wouldn't you agree?

## TREATMENT OF ANIMALS AND PLANTS

Although I have so far discussed using Reiki treatment of oneself and other people, you can also use Reiki to treat animals and plants. Reiki works on all living matter.

When I treat an animal, I notice that it relaxes and tends to be quiet. Cats love to curl up in your lap. They will often push up under your hands to feel the energy. You will soon notice that the Reiki energy flows into animals, just as it does into people. Use your imagination when working with different types of animals. You can put your hands on either side of an aquarium in order to treat fish. I have even worked with a snake – it curled up in my hands! A friend of mine in Scotland developed quite a reputation as a miracle worker. He was called out to look at a friend's horse. The horse was a steeplechase runner which had a lame foreleg and a problem with its shoulder. The vet said that he would have to be put out to pasture, because he would not be able to race again. However, Tom stood on a ladder to treat the horse's shoulder and then worked with its leg. After three treatments, the horse was fine and is still racing! Tom says he likes to work with four-legged animals, as they do not normally answer back. He took me to the stables one day to work with the animals. I was treating a horse when I heard

laughter. When I asked what was so funny, I was told that the horse had fallen asleep. I have always said that it is a compliment to the channel when the client falls asleep. This applies to animals too! Another woman that I know treats lambs. The vets call her to come and work with them out in the fields and mountains of Scotland. She is known to be quite a Reiki miracle worker.

I had an opportunity to treat my own dog, Schnapps. He had developed an incurable blood disease. The vet did not give him any hope at all. I took him home from the animal hospital every evening and treated him through the night. I slept with my hands on him. The vet was very surprised that the dog was responding and getting better. When he asked me what I was doing, I explained about Reiki. The vet took the Reiki course and is using it on his 'clients' successfully.

When using Reiki on plants, you can hold the pot in which they are planted between your hands. Hold seeds before you plant them in the ground and use Reiki to energize the water that you use to water them. I am always impressed at how strong and healthy plants are as a result of the treatments. When I am in nature, I hug trees and give them Reiki – but don't be surprised when the tree gives you back energy in return. There seems to be a giving and receiving when working with trees.

Above all, let your mind be free when you work with animals and plants: follow your intuition. Reiki is unlimited, with boundless energy going to all living matter. Reach out and touch – I promise that you will be pleasantly surprised!

## USING REIKI WITH DEATH AND DYING

I personally think that death is a part of transition, part of the never-ending cycle of rest and activity. We certainly have experiences of letting go in different ways. I have been honoured to be with people, loved ones, as they let go of the physical body, releasing the pain and struggle. They are at peace and filled with the loving energy of Reiki. It is a deeply moving experience for me. It seems as if they are more aware of themselves, the inner light within them, and are secure. Reiki is a gentle and effective means of supporting our loved ones, friends, and even animals, as they pass through this state of transition. Reiki can also be used to treat the family and friends through their grief process. It helps them to let go fully, with love.

Never doubt for a moment, or question whether Reiki is appropriate at this time. It is always the right time to reach out and touch, in all cases. You will be touched as well, by the love and gratitude you experience as an instrument of Reiki.

## ABSENT HEALING WITH SECOND DEGREE REIKI

Many people are surprised when they learn that Reiki can be sent to other people over long distances. It can hardly be surprising, once we realize that our bodies can act as receivers, just as a radio or television does for waves sent through the air. We are essentially wireless forms of transmission and receiving.

Natural laws exist which enable us to transfer life energy over long distances. The Reiki method of absent healing is based on these laws, and the key to them can be learned in the second degree of Reiki. It is not necessary to know all the natural laws in order to make use of this technique.

Absent healing is used when it is physically impossible to be with the person needing treatment. It is also a method which can be put to use immediately when you are asked to give treatment to someone. It can certainly be utilized to give additional treatment to a person you are working with in person. You can send them a nightly treatment to support them until you are together again.

If a person has never experienced Reiki, there may be a certain scepticism about the effect of this treatment.

My first experience in doing a treatment in this way was when I was taught absent healing by my Reiki Master. I worked on my daughter who, at the time, was many thousands of miles away, in Hawaii. I could find the various places of her body which needed treatment. I felt her presence with me during the entire time. Two days later, she telephoned and in the course of the conversation told me that she had been relieved of a headache and bad stomach-ache at the very time I had worked on her.

Quite recently, I was teaching in the Netherlands. During the seminar, I felt so lovingly supported and had a sense of warmth flooding my body. I later learned

that a Reiki support group made up of my students from Scotland had sent me absent healing at that same moment. Absent healing is indeed powerful and beautiful both for the therapist and the receiver – in this case, I was both.

Many times during second degree Reiki courses, I have asked my students to work on the planet Earth, or on a particular country in need of healing. It always fills us with love and gratitude that we can help our city, state, country and world with Reiki energy.

You should never treat a person by absent methods against their will. Everyone has the right to be healthy or unhealthy. It is best for the person needing the treatment to ask for it. If I am treating a person over a long time, I will ask for a photograph to work with, as well as their full name. I generally do absent healing in the evening, before I go to sleep. I find it a beautiful way to relax.

## MENTAL/EMOTIONAL RELEASE TECHNIQUE WITH SECOND DEGREE REIKI

We often react to negative experiences in our lives in such a manner that it programmes our minds to attract these stressful experiences into our lives time and time again. It makes us painfully right about our belief system. This reaction can also be the cause of our attachment to our resulting illness.

The mental/emotional release technique which is taught in the second degree of

Reiki, will enable you to release those attachments to that programmed part of you or another person, enabling the reactive energy to be set free.

Since most physical illness is derived from emotional/mental/spiritual disharmony, this method can be used for all disturbances and imbalances.

The instrument has a great deal of responsibility regarding the use of this technique: it should only be carried out with the full permission of the recipient, and you must take care not to project any judgements onto the person.

When I first went through this process, I released my attachment to someone who was no longer in my life. It was a profound experience. As a result of that experience, I felt able to move forward as 'Mari', unattached. I no longer felt incomplete without that person. This was a major turning point in my life.

One of my translators for the courses in the Czech Republic said that it seemed too easy to work. Yet as the days went by, she noticed that the fear she had when encountering large groups of people had disappeared. This is what she had worked on removing. She is now quite comfortable with large groups, and her personality has changed as she gains in self-confidence.

Reaction is turned into response. As we respond to life, we are able to be objective and go with the flow, rather than being in that reactive and subjective state where we experience being stuck in a situation …We are free!

# Using Reiki with Other Healing Techniques

Reiki supports and increases the effectiveness of every form of treatment that I know of. Many people combine their existing knowledge and training with Reiki: medical doctors, physiotherapists, psychotherapists, chiropractors and masseurs. People use Reiki with acupuncture, acupressure, colour therapy, crystal healing, homeopathy, breath work, bioenergetics and mind-directed energy.

I myself have used Reiki with several other healing techniques that I have learned, with successful results. Recently, I have studied with a Polish healer in his country. He has people coming to him from all over the world. He taught me mind-directed healing methods. We can see how this energy and the energy of Reiki come together, increasing the effectiveness of both. We worked with people together, and the recipients reported to me their experiences with the combined energy. I have been very fortunate to have had this experience.

Reiki is always the basis. Do not be afraid to experiment with ways in which Reiki can enhance whatever other form of treatment you use, or that you are studying. Reiki is yours to use and will become unique to you as the instrument, as it is combined with whatever other techniques you use, enhancing your work and yourself.

There are many types of harmonizing techniques. In this chapter, I shall deal with a few of them and the ways in which Reiki can be integrated with them to promote harmony. In no way do I claim to be an authority on these techniques, but I have found their use beneficial to my Reiki work.

# REIKI WITH SOUND (TONING)

Sound is vibration and our bodies react and respond to different frequencies, or tones. People have their own unique vibrational or base tone, as well as a tone in each of the chakras. We are surrounded by sound: some sounds support us, others sounds can create imbalance. Sound has been used for healing for centuries by people from various traditions and cultures. Many contemporary healers use toning to alter the energetic field of their clients to improve harmony and health. Different tones and tone combinations can be used for different purposes, such as loosening energy blocks and charging the aura of the body and the chakras. You can, as you are transmitting Reiki energy, also tone into the chakra to increase the energy flow and increase the harmonizing effect. Generally, you can work with a scale of G, as it is the tone that resonates with the earth.

Below is a guideline for the notes of the musical scale to be used with each chakra, and also the colour vibration that is produced with each note. To harmonize each chakra, always trust your intuition about which note to use.

## COLOUR THERAPY WITH REIKI

Every colour has its own vibration. Colour is essential to health and we are often attracted to the colours we need to promote balance. Surely, every disease is associated with dysfunction in the chakras. Chakras can be nourished with the colours in which they are lacking. A chakra can be energized with the required

| CHAKRA | | COLOUR | TONE |
|---|---|---|---|
| 7th | crown | white | G |
| 6th | third eye | purple | D |
| 5th | throat | blue | A |
| 4th | heart | green | G |
| 3rd | solar plexus | yellow | F |
| 2nd | sacral | orange | D |
| 1st | root | red | G (below C ) |

colour and the effect increased with Reiki energy. Because every colour has a diiferent vibration, we will have a different reaction or response to each one. Some colours naturally make us feel more open and expanded, while others make us feel more contracted. We may also be reacting in a certain way because we are associating a colour with a previous personal experience. In the United States many hospital rooms used to be painted pale green. Since I spent long months in hospitals, I naturally had an aversion to that colour. Now, after a wide variety of studies on the healing effect of colour, those hospital rooms are being painted in different colour tones.

Our relationship to colour can also be an expression of what is happening in our energy fields as a result of an emotional reaction and mental decision to a situation or event. For example, if our first and second chakras are not balanced, the emotional reaction registered in our energy field is perhaps that we have lost our will to live and also our sexuality. By wearing red or orange to balance that chakra, it may bring forth emotional issues that are blocking the area, thus allowing the area to be cleared. Perhaps we have an underactive thyroid: blue supports the balancing and harmonizing of the throat centre as it expands. If the thyroid is overactive you can use green to balance the area, as perhaps there is too much blue in that centre. When working with colour there are no strict rules, but generally the chakras respond well to the following colours by chakra:

### FIRST CHAKRA (ROOT) — RED AND BLACK

Red increases your connection to the earth and strengthens the basic will to live in the physical world. It is the colour of passion and will, good for all organs in root chakra area and the legs. Black helps you to come within yourself and be centered. It is a more masculine energy and can be like coming back into the womb or the void to find deep, internal creative forces. If used well, it can support and strengthen you. Overuse can bring depression. It is good for healing the bones.

### SECOND CHAKRA (SACRAL) — ORANGE

Orange stimulates the sexual energy and enhances the immune system. It increases your ambition and is good for all the organs in the sacral area. It also opens you to your creative expression.

### THIRD CHAKRA (SOLAR PLEXUS) — YELLOW

Yellow is good for mental clarity and a sense of what is just or fair. It is a warming soothing colour, like sunshine, and is good for all organs in the solar plexus area.

## FOURTH CHAKRA (HEART) — GREEN OR ROSE

Green promotes a strong active love for others, and healing for heart and lung problems. It helps you to love. Green embodies the balance and fullness of love — everything is fine with me, you and the world; and nurturing — think of Mother Nature. It is especially good for the heart and lungs and all the organs connected to the heart centre. Pink represents a soft, yielding love for others.

## FIFTH CHAKRA (THROAT) — BLUE

Blue helps you to speak the truth, increases your sensitivity, strengthens the inner teacher and brings peace, truth and a quiet sense of order. It is wonderful for all issues of trust. Dark blue helps put you in touch with a deeper sense of purpose and is good for all the organs in the throat chakra area.

## SIXTH CHAKRA (THIRD EYE) — PURPLE

Purple opens up spiritual perception, brings a feeling of ecstasy, and deepens your spiritual life. Purple promotes integration and movement into spiritual awareness, and carries a sense of royalty. It increases your sense of leadership and respect. Lavender promotes a lighthearted attitude to others and life. Purple encourages a feeling of 'lightness', and supports all the organs and glands in the third eye area.

## SEVENTH CHAKRA (CROWN) — WHITE, GOLD AND SILVER

White helps connect you to your purity and innocence. It brings spiritual expansion and connection to others on a spiritual plane. It reduces pain and is very good for the brain. Gold enhances the higher mind and your connection to God and the spiritual strength in you. It strengthens all parts of the body and has a masculine energy. Silver helps you to move faster and communicate better — 'quicksilver' (feminine energy).

Of course, there are many colours and tones of colour — always trust your intuition in choosing. You can place a coloured square of material or paper over the area of a chakra. Place your Reiki hand on top of the coloured square, sending the energy through the colour into the area. Using this method accelerates and deepens the balancing effect. If you have been attuned to Reiki Two energy, you can use that energy when working with colour.

You can also use the seven basic colours — red, orange, yellow, green, blue, purple and white — on the seven chakras and energize the crown chakra, using Position 2 for the head (see page 57). The energy goes through both sides of the brain, bringing about integration, and continues down the body to produce harmony in the entire body.

Use colour in your everyday life for harmony. Choose colours for your clothing and the rooms of your living space that promote inner peace and balance.

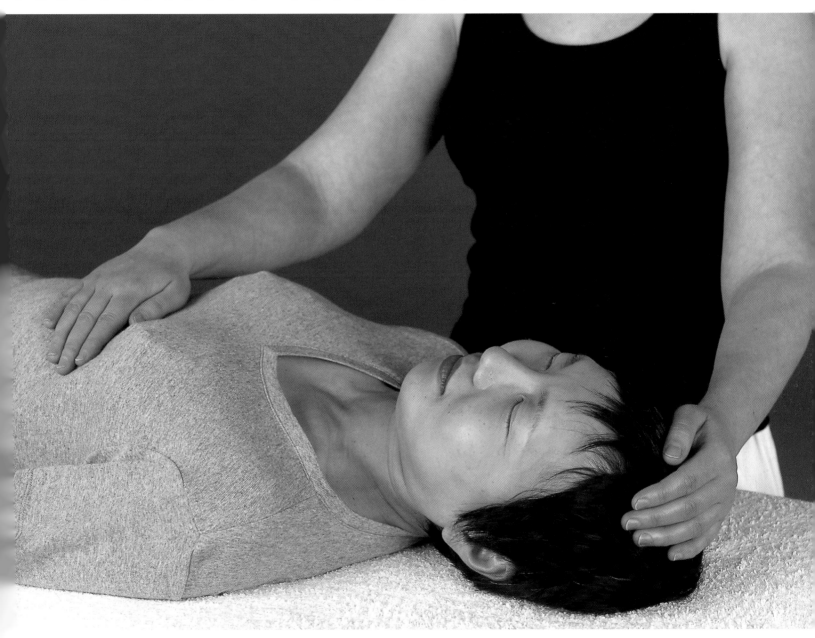

## REIKI WITH CRYSTALS

Crystals have different vibrational qualities, as well as colours. You can energize the balancing effect of crystals with Reiki. By placing your hand directly over the crystal as it is lying on the body, the healing effect is intensified. Each crystal has its own harmonizing effect and they are generally used in the area of the chakra. Remember that, ultimately, it is your intuitive nature that will guide you where to place the stones. Trust yourself and your Reiki hands. Of course, more than one stone can be used in any one area. I have found it beneficial to spend quiet time in meditation with each stone, to feel its vibration and to develop my own relationship with each one, before I use the crystals on other people. As to the cleansing of stones, there are many schools of thought. I use a simple prayer with each stone, saying, 'I dedicate you to the light of Christ. I programme you to be self-cleansing and to work for the highest good of all mankind.' Once you have completed a Reiki Two seminar, you can use the symbols from Reiki Two to clean the crystals. Crystals love the sunlight and like to be bathed and cleansed just like us. Some basic stones and their healing properties are listed below, by chakra.

## CROWN CHAKRA

### Clear Quartz

Clear quartz improves the crystalline characteristics of the blood, body and mind. It activates and improves the functioning of the brain and is excellent for meditation. It works with all the chakras.

Milk quartz (white) helps with milk production, enhances bones and teeth and works with the entire body and all seven chakras.

## THIRD EYE CHAKRA

### Amethyst

Amethyst has calming, strong protective qualities and is useful for inspiration and intuition. It strengthens the immune and endocrine systems and works on the third eye and crown chakras. It also enhances right brain activity and the functioning of the pineal and pituitary glands. It is one of the best stones for meditation and has an excellent calming effect.

## THROAT CHAKRA

### Blue Agate

Blue agate on the throat chakra it helps us to express truly our thoughts and feelings, both conscious and subconscious. This stone is also good for counter-action of red energies like passion, infections, inflammations and fevers. It empowers the whole organism, especially the body and mind and gives the strength of goodness, courage, trust and clear communication. It also helps to clear away frustration and lassitude and is useful for eye illnesses and breathing and nerve problems.

### Lapis lazuli

This stone is used for mental and spiritual cleansing. It strengthens the skeletal system, and activates the thyroid gland, thus releasing tension and anxiety. It encourages mental clarity and illumination, thus enhancing psychic ability and is good for creative expression. It works with the throat and third eye chakras.

### Sodalite

Sodalite strengthens the metabolism and lymphatic system, and balances the masculine/feminine polarities. It aids the pancreas and balances the endocrine system. It calms and clears the mind, thus alleviating fear. It cuts through density and illusion, bringing clarity and truth. It enhances communication and creative expression. It is slightly grounding and acts like a sedative. It works with the throat and third eye chakras.

### Turquoise

Turquoise attunes and empowers the whole body. It helps with the circulation of air and blood in the lungs, which in turn strengthens the whole respiratory system. It vitalizes the blood and stabilizes the nervous system. It is used for balancing the mind during meditation, and for promoting constructive expression, communication, friendship and loyalty. It is great for expressing the truth in every form and for encouraging a person to listen to their inner voice.

## HEART CHAKRA

### Aventurine

Green aventurine is used for many kinds of illness on the mental, emotional and physical levels. It is good for the heart, as it counteracts emotions and gives greater balance to the physical body. Aventurine crystals are recommended to wear when a person is stressed. Put aventurine near to the heart and solar plexus chakras to release deep emotional trauma and soothe stress. It strengthens the blood and stimulates muscle tissue.

### Chrysopras

Chrysopras is a member of the quartz family which moderates neurotic problems and depression. It harmonizes sexual imbalance. When used or directed to the heart chakra it dispels pain and sadness and brings inner peace. Chrysopras bolsters hormone regulation during the menstrual cycle and is good to use during pregnancy. It is also great for men to use, to help them with the ability to feel and heal emotional problems. It works with the heart and sacral chakras.

### Malachite

Malachite aids the functions of the pancreas and spleen. It reduces stress and tension and aids sleep. It promotes tissue regeneration, and strengthens the heart, circulatory system, pineal and pituitary glands. It reveals subconscious blocks and vitalizes the body and mind. It works with the heart and solar plexus chakras.

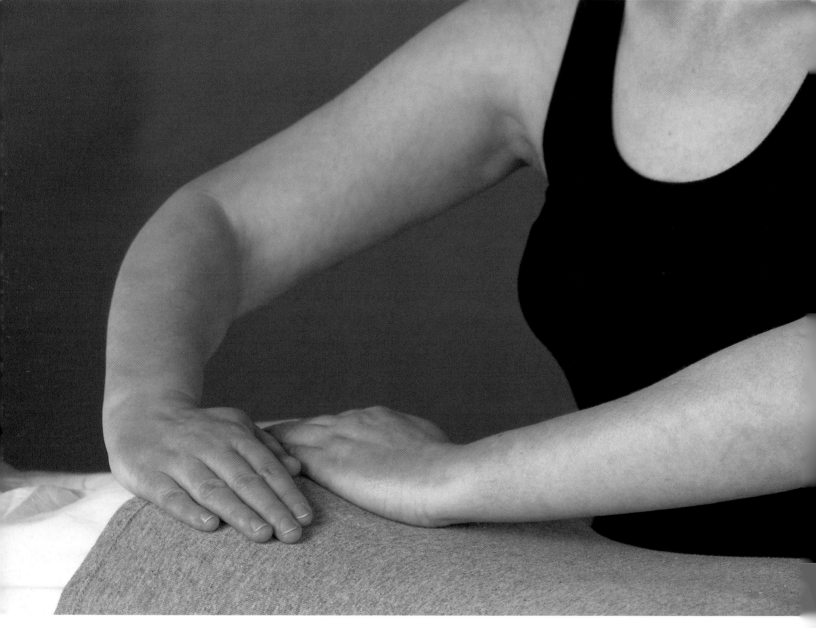

### Rhodochrosite

Rhodochrosite acts as a bridge for the heart, solar plexus and root centres, enabling the person to have a clear capacity for selfless love and compassion. As the bridging of these chakras takes place, the person is empowered to utilize their full creative potential. It works well with Malachite to clear and balance the chakras. An emotional balancer, helping to heal emotional wounds and traumas, it also aids the spleen, kidneys, heart, prostrate gland and the circulation of the blood. The pink/red colour helps to blend the courage and passion of the root chakra with the loving expression of the heart. It is for divine love, and acceptance of yourself and your life. It works with the root, solar plexus and heart chakras.

### Rose quartz

Rose quartz is a member of the quartz family that has a beautiful soft vibration and great healing potential. It promotes peace with its soft colour vibration. It helps to clear stored anger, resentment, fear and jealousy. It helps kidneys and the circulation, increases fertility, calms sexual and emotional imbalance and helps to clear accumulated anger. It also aids the development of forgiveness, compassion and love and works with the heart chakra.

*After we can truly love ourselves we are able to love others without any prejudices.*
MARI HALL

## SOLAR PLEXUS CHAKRA

### Citrine

Citrine is great to use when we are trying to be successful in creativity, education and interrelationships. It brings the power of golden light into the material dimension of real life. It is excellent for the kidneys, liver, gall bladder, colon, all the digestive organs and the heart. Citrine can be used for tissue regeneration and is a detoxifier for the physical, emotional and mental aspects. It helps one to see clearly into one's personal problems and alleviates depression to bring about a sense of light-heartedness. It works with the crown and solar plexus chakras.

### Tiger's eye

Tiger's eye is beneficial for the spleen, pancreas and digestive organs, has a grounding and centring effect that is slightly masculine in polarity and works with the sacral and solar plexus chakras. If you put tiger's eye on the solar plexus chakra, you can direct high energy coming into the body to this area and create a sense of well-being.

### Topaz

Topaz enhances our connection to the Earth. This stone ties God or the Creative Power into human acts, illuminating the higher self. It vitalizes the liver, gall, spleen, digestive organs and the nervous system and extracts impurities from the body. It works with the crown, solar plexus and root chakras.

## SACRAL CHAKRA

### *Carnelian*

Carnelian is used for grounding energy and is great for preoccupied people, or those who cannot concentrate and even get flustered. It focuses attention on the present moment, thus helping a person to concentrate better and be more productive. In meditation, it helps one to concentrate on higher goals. Its red-orange colour stimulates sexual energy and helps to clean blood in the reproductive organs. It empowers potency and pregnancy. It stops bleeding and decreases fever, energizes the blood, helps with kidney activation, and with tissue regeneration in the lungs, liver, pancreas and gall. It works with the heart and root chakras.

## ROOT CHAKRA

### *Blood Jaspis*

Blood jaspis is a strong instrument for cleansing the physical body. Jaspis cleans the blood and vitalizes the organs involved with the kidneys, liver and spleen. For people who have been through mental or physical problems, jaspis can provide increased light and energy. It strengthens the heart, spleen and marrow of the bone, by energizing and oxygenating the bloodstream. It enhances physical and mental vitality and reduces emotional and psychological stress. It works with the heart and root chakras.

### Obsidian

Obsidian is good for emotional people with a tendency to be distant, because it stabilizes unstable energies. Obsidian is like a mirror that reflects mistakes and increases fears, insecurities and temptations to be self-centred that impede the higher soul qualities. It supports the stomach and intestines, absorbs and eradicates negative energy and is good for the reduction of stress. Masculine in nature, it works with the root chakra.

### Hematite

Hematite enhances personal magnetism, optimism, well-being and courage. It is good to use after an operation, as well as for shocks, traumas and stressful situations. Hematite can help people who have sleeping problems or who suffer from nightmares. Place the stone under your pillow to ground and stabilize the etheric body while sleeping. It has a direct effect on the bloodstream and is excellent for the kidneys. It activates the spleen, increases resistance to stress, helps with oxygen circulation and works with the root chakra.

## REIKI WITH MEDITATION AND OTHER HARMONIZING TECHNIQUES

There are a variety of meditation practices, which are all beneficial to the individual. If I want clear vision into a problem with the stillness of my mind, I place my hands over the third eye area to energize and harmonize my intuition. If I am meditating on a question regarding trust and/or communication, I place my hand

at the throat centre. Not only does the hand provide a focus, the energy actually helps the chakra to clear, thus enabling answers to come forward. I truly believe that the heart is our centre of knowing and that all our experiences are integrated through the heart centre. It is for this reason that I will often meditate with my hands on the heart centre. However you choose to integrate Reiki into your meditation, I am sure your experience will be enhanced.

Reiki can be used with any technique for harmonizing. It has been my personal experience to use Reiki with sound, colour, crystals, homeopathy, nutrition, flower remedies, acupressure, reflexology, psychological and spiritual counselling, regression therapy, massage, whole brain re-education, bioenergetics and psychotronics. You, as an individual, will take the best of what you experience and already know and combine it with Reiki to make it uniquely yours. Above all, we should realize that we are only the vehicle for divine unconditional love and that everything else is like the flavourings or seasonings that are added to it. It is my hope that, should you choose Reiki as a pathway for yourself, you also continue to find out more about yourself and our world using different techniques. Ultimately, all things are part of the greater whole, as we are one with all things in our world.

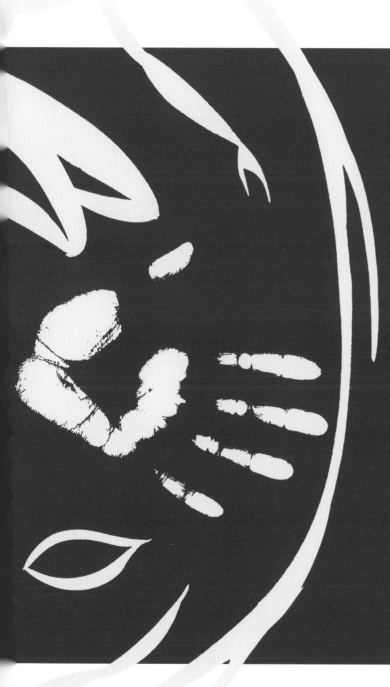

# The
# Endocrine
# System
# and the
# Chakras

In their teachings, Dr Usui and Hawayo Takata stressed the importance of harmony in the endocrine system and of balancing the chakras.

## THE CHAKRAS AND THEIR CORRESPONDING ENDOCRINE GLANDS

| 7th Chakra | Crown | Hypothalamus |
|---|---|---|
| 6th Chakra | Third eye | Pituitary |
| 5th Chakra | Throat | Thyroid and four parathyroids |
| 4th Chakra | Heart | Thymus |
| 3rd Chakra | Solar plexus | Adrenals (cortex medulla) |
| 2nd Chakra | Sacral/base | Testes in males, ovaries in females |
| 1st Chakra | Root | Adrenals |

Although our endocrine glands have specific individual functions and work independently, overactivity or underactivity of one gland will affect the entire system. These ductless glands produce hormones, which are chemical messengers that pass into the bloodstream and circulation to stimulate or inhibit activity of other organs and tissue. Hormones regulate important processes of the body, such as metabolism, growth, ageing, maintenance of stability of the internal environment (homeostasis), the body's ability to heal itself, resistance to stress and reproduction. Some other systems also produce hormones that are passed into the bloodstream: the digestive system produces gastrin in the stomach; enterogastrone, secretin, cholecystokinin and pancreozymin in the small intestine; and erthropoietin and rennin in the kidney.

The hand positions used in Reiki correspond to the location of the major endocrine glands in the body. The glands work together in harmony. Stress is the major inhibitor to the harmony of the body's metabolism. Full body treatments with Reiki reduce stress, allowing the body to heal itself naturally.

When using hand positions on the head, the energy is directly influencing the pineal and pituitary glands. The pineal gland is the major gland controlling the amount of light that is brought into the body, and regulates sexual development and skin pigmentation. The pituitary gland enhances the state of the mind; regulates sleep, growth and body fluids; works to sharpen the senses of smell and taste; and encourages the body to replace dead cells.

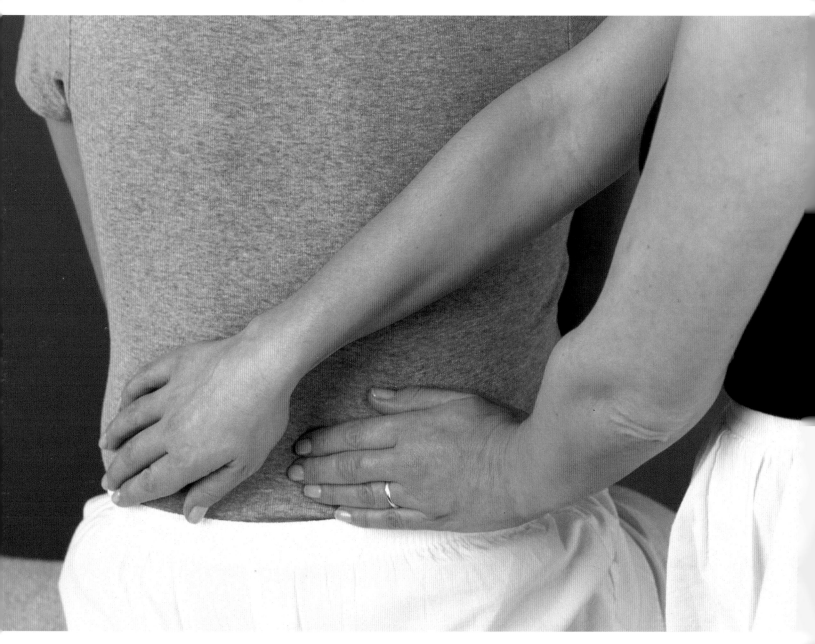

When you are using the hand positions over the throat area, the energy is directly influencing the thyroid gland, which regulates the rate at which we burn up food and the rate of intensity at which we live. It keeps the iodine level correct in our body, regulates the mucous membranes, aids digestion and builds nerve and brain tissue. The energy also affects the parathyroid glands, which regulate calcium levels in our bodies and promotes a sense of calm.

As we move our hands further down, the energy will directly influence the thymus gland, which is also called the 'transpersonal heart'. The thymus gland produces 'T'-cells, one of the primary agents for the body to defend itself against disease. Dis-ease also corresponds to our state of mind.

When our hands are placed over the kidneys, the energy is also directly influencing the adrenal glands, which stimulate our sexuality and creativity. They give us energy and stamina and good muscle tone. When working over the reproductive areas the energy directly affects our sexual glands and regulates fertility and our emotional states.

The system works beautifully when it is harmonized. We feel alive and happy!

## THE CHAKRAS AND THEIR RELATED FUNCTION IN THE BODY

Chakras are energy centres and serve as gateways for the flow of energy and life into the physical body. Each chakra is associated with the glands and organs in that part of the body. They react and respond to energy and vibration. The energy flow of the chakra can be in disharmony as result of imbalance or stress in the emotional, mental or spiritual aspect of an individual. This disharmony can eventually cause physical illness. The chakras can be balanced by placing your hand on the energy centre. This will bring about a release of the blocked energy, and a harmonizing effect takes place. When all the chakras are balanced, the chakras will feel the same.

I am giving you some information about the chakras. I have listed their location; function; the emotional energy associated with them; how we block the energy (our thoughts); the resulting body language indicating an imbalance in the area; organs and body functions controlled by the energies; and what kind of disease or illness will occur if there is imbalance. In the succeeding chapter, I will discuss further the emotional causes of illness, by chakra.

*The Chakras*

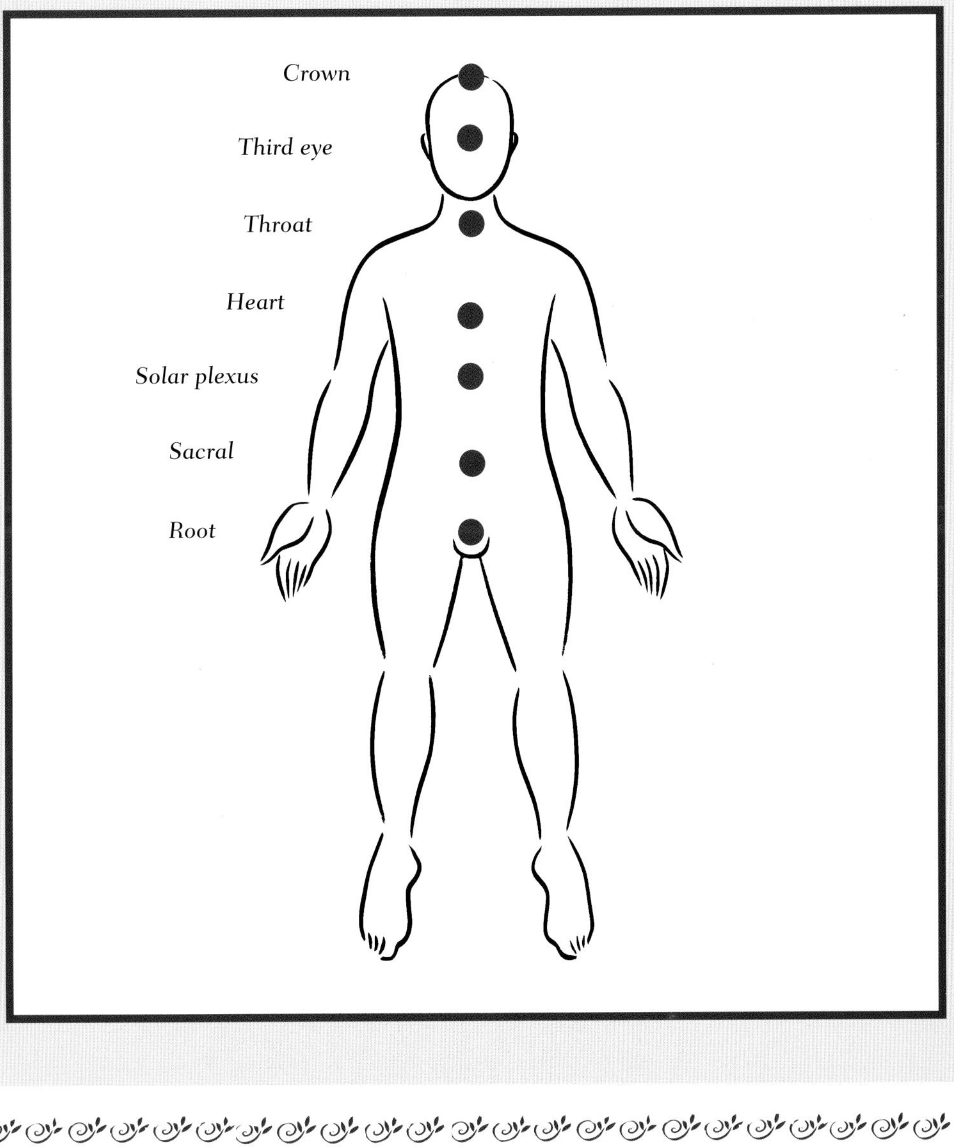

Crown

Third eye

Throat

Heart

Solar plexus

Sacral

Root

# The Energy Centres

## I ROOT CHAKRA (MULADHARA)

| | |
|---|---|
| Location: | Where sacrum joins coccyx, in rear, to middle bottom of pubic bone, in front. |
| Function: | Seat of Kundalini energy; creative expression, abundance. |
| Emotional energy: | Survival; power; aggression; contact with the earth; the will to live; being active in the world; confidence; strength; self-acceptance; vitality; 'fight or flight' responses. |
| Blocks to these energies: | Fear of being in the world; feeling threatened in the above areas. |
| Body language: | Crossing our legs: our legs look all twisted up like a spiral. |
| These energies control: | Adrenal glands; kidneys; spine; joint controller of the bladder; affects the whole nervous system. |
| Diseases: | Problems of the legs, hips and buttocks. |

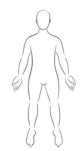

# 2 SACRAL CHAKRA (SVADHISTANA)

| | |
|---|---|
| Location: | Between the pubic bone and navel. |
| Function: | Centre of sexual energy; feeling/emotional centre. |
| Emotional energy: | Sexuality; sensuality; personal creativity; nourishment; family ties; social behaviour patterns; sensitivity; social consciousness. |
| Blocks to these energies: | Feeling threatened in the above areas; lack of self-acceptance, self-love and self-esteem. |
| Body language: | Sitting with hip area back in chair and leaning forward; standing with hands clasped in front or behind. |
| These energies control: | The gonads (ovaries and testes); fluid functions of the body. |
| Diseases: | Reproductive disorders; pre-menstrual tension and irregular periods in women; impotence in both sexes; bowel and bladder problems; AIDS. |

# 3 SOLAR PLEXUS OR POWER CENTRE (MANI PURA)

Location:                    Between the navel and base of the rib cage.
Function:                    Power and wisdom centre.
Emotional energy:            Connections and attachments to people and things; love in attachment – dependency; relationship to the environment; draws in energy; expels stress; 'gut' feelings about people.
Blocks to these energies: Fears or anxieties about anything 'out there'.
Body language:               Hands/arms over stomach area; legs crossed, elbows on knees; things on lap; hands hooked in belt.
These energies control:  Adrenals; stomach; liver; gall bladder; the digestive system.
Diseases:                    Repressed energy at cell level, often leading to cancer; arthritis; problems with the above organs ('butterflies', constipation, diarrhoea, ulcers, digestive problems); migraines; heart disease in relation to our fear of power.

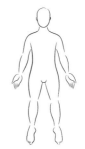

# 4 HEART CHAKRA (ANAHATA)

| | |
|---|---|
| Location: | Centre of the chest – sternum. |
| Function: | Love, compassion. |
| Emotional energy: | The whole: holistic thinking; impersonal feelings and unconditional love; healing centre; humility; responsibility; goodwill; tolerance; empathy and compassion. (The solar plexus is selective and determines what you see – linked to one's belief system. The heart is inclusive and sees 'what is' – it picks up the soul quality of a person). |
| Blocks to these energies: | The biggest aspect of the heart is unconditional love and trust of others. Therefore, blockages come from fear caused by old emotional hurts; lack of emotional security; fear of letting others in; and protection from recurrence of past hurts. |
| Body language: | Arms folded; one arm across chest – holding books etc. |
| These energies control: | Thymus gland; heart; blood pressure/circulation; the whole immune system; lungs. |
| Diseases: | Heart attack; problems with blood pressure; problems of the circulatory system; immune system disease (AIDS). |

## 5 THROAT CHAKRA (VISHUDDA)

| | |
|---|---|
| Location: | Throat area. |
| Function: | Communication. |
| Emotional energy: | Creativity; self-expression; productivity; personal aliveness; individuality; action; desire for peace over conflict; trust of ourselves and others. |
| Blocks to these energies: | Stifling of the above; rigidity; unwillingness to compromise; frustrated communication. |
| Body language: | Coughs – clearing throat; wearing collar and tie, heavy necklaces etc.; hands on chin. |
| These energies control: | Thyroid gland; voice; oesophagus; neck; lower jaw; strongly linked with sacral chakra. |
| Diseases: | Diseases of the throat and lungs. |

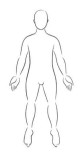

# 6 THIRD EYE OR BROW CHAKRA (AJNA)

| | |
|---|---|
| Location: | 2.5cm (1 inch) above centre of eyebrows. |
| Function: | Intuitive centre; seat of will and clairvoyance. |
| Emotional energy: | Left hemisphere function (rational mind); integrated personality balance; planning; will; purpose; control; self-control; ambition; choice; assertiveness; telepathy; super-ego – injunctions of parents; programmed actions. Right hemisphere function (creative mind); creative and artistic nature, the gentle, receptive, and intuitive. It represents our relationship with feminine nature. |
| Blocks to these energies: | Confusion in any of the above areas. |
| Body language: | Wiping, rubbing and tapping of brow; hand on forehead when studying; furrowed brow when confused; eyes wide open when we have realized something profound. |
| These energies control: | Pituitary gland – the master gland, controlling and balancing all the other glands; nose; ears; sinuses; autonomic nervous system (with root chakra); hypothalamus; lower brain. Diseases: Diseases of the autonomic nervous system; hormonal imbalance; headaches; migraines; sinusitis; dizziness; depression; eye/ear problems. |

# 7 CROWN CHAKRA (SAHASRARA)

| | |
|---|---|
| Location: | Top (crown) of the head. |
| Function: | Connects us to our spiritual self. |
| Emotional energy: | Transpersonal awareness; the whole; systems; connectedness; relatedness; inner development; consciousness; unity with all things. |
| Blocks to these energies: | Feeling cut off; alone (aloneness versus 'All-one-ness'); as all other centres come into balance, they are activated in the crown. |
| Body language: | Hands over head; stroking hair back; hats; various religious practices of covering or shaving this chakra; crowns on kings and queens as a symbol of opening this centre and of unity with all things. |
| These energies control: | Pineal gland (this gland is light sensitive, and is very active from birth until about seven years; secretes melatonin); time issues; circadian rhythms – jet lag effects. |
| Diseases: | Serious psychotic disorders; being totally cut off, as in severe grief; deeply hurt people in psychiatric institutions; deep shock; inability to face reality. |

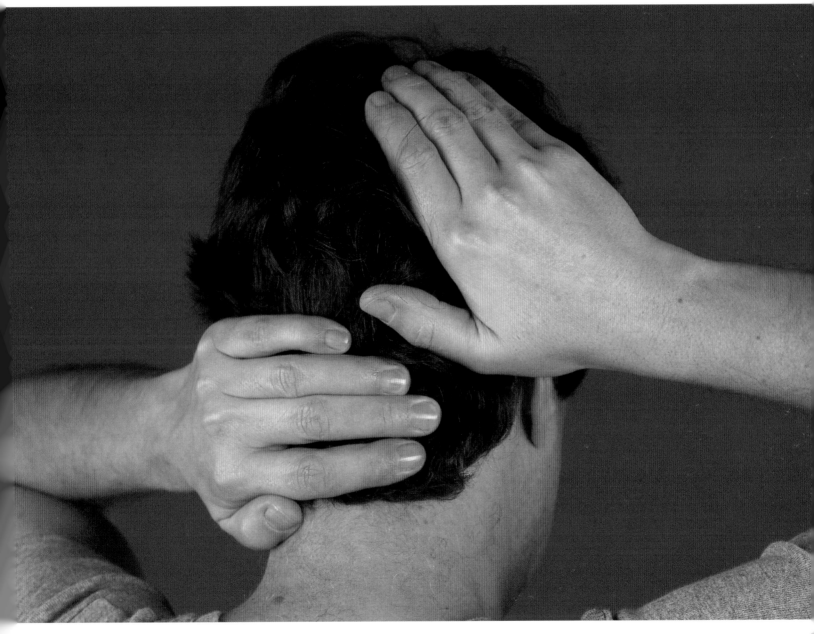
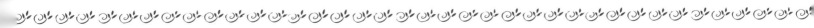

# Probable Emotional Causes of Illness, by Chakra

It is almost impossible to divide symptoms into individual chakras, as illness is interrelated. I have attempted to show you that, in each area, there is probable resulting illness. There are many more illnesses than those indicated, and many of these involve more than one chakra. Illness occurs when the energy is blocked in one or more of the centres. We should always look at ourselves and other people as whole beings: physical, emotional, mental and spiritual, with the symptoms manifesting on different levels. It is safe to say that Reiki addresses the causes, as well as the resulting illness. This chapter is a way of looking at yourself and others to see what the emotional causes of your problems could be.

Again, illness is the result of an imbalance, usually caused by a mental decision, based on an emotional reaction to an event or events in our lives. Once the mind is made up, then your life becomes an adventure of discovering how right your mind is, and experiencing the resulting illness which can, and usually does, occur.

Your mind is a powerful tool, which can work for and against you and your well-being. Reiki will enable you to clear the mind and open your heart to love and health.

This is in no way an attempt to list every illness or symptom of illness. It is merely a guide. Ask yourself: 'What are my thoughts and fears?', 'What am I not expressing, and how is this manifesting itself physically in me at this moment?' Your answers are always there inside you.

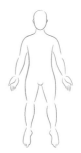

### I ROOT CHAKRA — OUR STABILITY AND SEAT OF PHYSICAL VITALITY

Varicose veins
Usually indicates unhappiness in our choice of work; we feel overworked and overburdened.

Legs
Problems with the legs indicate fear of moving forward into life. If the upper leg is involved, it usually has something to do with past childhood trauma, which is keeping us stuck in a situation.

Kidney problems
Critical of yourself; a feeling of shame and disappointment in your life and in yourself. This is the place we store our 'pissed off' energy and anger. Problems in this area usually indicate that this has not been expressed.

Knees
Knee problems are usually associated with our inability to be flexible, and involves our pride and ego.

Hips
Fear about going forward with major decisions; also the feeling of being unloved, and harbouring resentment.

Buttocks
This is a power or powerless indicator: soft buttocks can mean a loss of power.

Sciatic centre
Is usually concerned with being hypocritical; also a fear about money and the future. Holding on to fear keeps you from moving forward.

Anus
Can indicate guilt over the past and unwillingness to release the pain of it all.

### 2 SACRAL CHAKRA — OUR CENTRE FOR SEXUAL ENERGY

| | |
|---|---|
| Lower back | Pain in this area usually means that you are not feeling supported financially. |
| Slipped disc | Feeling out on a limb, not supported by others in your life. |
| Appendicitis | Can mean that you are afraid of life and are blocking the flow of good energy. |
| Bladder problems | Holding on to old ideas, fearful of letting go; can also accompany anxiety. |
| Constipation | Stuck in the past; refusing to release old ideas and move on to something new. |
| Diarrhoea | Fear and rejection of things that may nourish you. |
| Female problems | A rejection of your femininity, associated with guilt and fear; can be a denial of your sexual energy. |
| Fibroid tumours/cysts | Usually occur after receiving a shock or extreme blow to your feminine ego. |
| Frigidity | Fear of pleasure: what will happen to you if you enjoy sex? Perhaps, also, insensitive partners. |
| Menstrual Cramps | You could be holding on to fear, thus creating tension in this area. |
| Miscarriage | Fear of the future – perhaps feeling it is not the right time; you are not ready on some level. |
| Pubic bone | Problems in this area usually involve genital protection. |

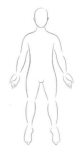

| | |
|---|---|
| Sterility | Fear and resistance to the process of life, and not trusting because of the fear. |
| Testicles | Represents the masculine energy and problems could result from a fear and rejection of this energy. |
| Vaginitis | Usually means that you are punishing yourself over sexual guilt, or that you are angry at your partner. |
| Venereal disease | Sexual guilt; in all cases of venereal disease, there will be an abstinence from sex and self-punishment. |
| Urinary infections | Usually being angry at the opposite sex or a lover, and blaming others. |

### 3 SOLAR PLEXUS CHAKRA — OUR EGO CENTRE

| | |
|---|---|
| Adrenal glands | A feeling of being defeated, so that you no longer care for yourself. |
| Abdominal cramps | There is a fear, so you are stopping the process. |
| Appetite problems | Always fear; if you are eating excessively, you are feeling the necessity to protect yourself and are judging your emotions – eating instead of expressing; if you have a loss of appetite, you are usually not trusting life, and do not feel that you deserve to be nourished. |
| Belching | Fear that there will not be enough, so that you gulp life too quickly. |
| Diabetes | Holding on to deep sorrow, so that there is no sweetness left in life; also, a great need to control. |

| | |
|---|---|
| Fat/overweight | Probably running away from your feelings and protecting yourself; oversensitive to life. |
| Gallstones | So much bitterness and hard feelings that you have developed a condemning pride. |
| Gas Pains | These are usually undigested ideas, and you are gripped with fear. |
| Gastritis | Living with a sense of doom and prolonged uncertainty. |
| Indigestion | You have anxiety and dread; fear at the gut level. |
| Liver | This is the seat of anger and primitive emotions. Problems in this area usually indicate anger that has not been expressed. |
| Nausea | Fear and rejecting ideas and experiences. |
| Peptic ulcers | Fear and an overwhelming desire to please others, so that you become anxious. |
| Spleen | Being obsessed with things. |
| Stomach problems | Fear and dread that you do not have the ability to assimilate something new and unknown. |
| Arthritis | Overcritical and resentful; feeling unloved. |

## 4 HEART CHAKRA — OUR CENTRE FOR UNCONDITIONAL LOVE

| | |
|---|---|
| Asthma | Having the experience of being smothered by love; suppressed crying and the feeling of being stifled; you cannot breathe for yourself. |

| | |
|---|---|
| Anxiety | You are probably not trusting the flow of life and its processes. |
| Arteries | The arteries carry the joy of life: you are not allowing the full expression of joy in your life. |
| Back | Upper – stuck in all that 'stuff', needing to say 'get off my back'; feeling burdened. Middle – feeling emotionally unsupported and unloved, and also not giving out love, holding on. |
| Blood | The blood represents the free flowing joy in your life. |
| Breasts | This is the mothering and nurturing aspect: you could be over-mothering, or have a fear of being nurtured or mothered yourself. |
| Lungs | Problems in this area usually mean that you have stopped receiving and lost the ability to take in life. Breathing problems represent the refusal to take life in. Pneumonia means that you are tired of life, and desperate. These are emotions that you are not allowing yourself to heal. |
| Heartburn | There is so much fear in your life, that it is as if it is clutching your heart. |
| Heart imbalance | The heart is the centre for love and security; you are probably lacking joy, and have squeezed the joy out of your life; also indicates inability to love yourself and others. |

## 5 THROAT CHAKRA — OUR CENTRE FOR TRUST AND COMMUNICATION

Bad breath
Contained thoughts of anger and revenge. Your experiences are blocked up and stale.

Blood pressure
High – usually means long-standing emotional problems which have not been solved. Low – not feeling that you were loved as a child; a defeated attitude – giving up, as in 'What's the use?'

Bronchial problems
Problems with receiving: breathing problems indicate a refusal to take in life fully.

Bronchitis
Results from the family environment; an inflamed situation, and not expressing your sorrow.

Hay fever
Emotionally congested with feelings of guilt.

Hypertension
You have probably been fulfilling the needs of others, and forgetting about yourself; disappointed that you cannot do what you want to.

Influenza
This is your reaction to mass negativity and the fear around and inside of you.

Jaw problems
There is so much resentment and anger, with a desire for revenge, that you become rigid.

Neck problems
Your inflexibility and stubbornness have given you a pain in the neck.

Nose problems
A crying out for love, and the need for self-recognition.

Teeth problems
Feeling indecisive over a long time.

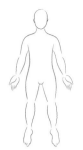

| | |
|---|---|
| Throat | Having the inability to speak up for yourself; swallowed anger, stifled creativity and the refusal to change. |
| Tonsillitis | Fear and repressed emotion; lack of trust of others or the future. |
| Thyroid problems | A feeling of being humiliated: 'not what I wanted to do', 'when will it be my turn?' |

## 6 THIRD EYE CHAKRA (BROW) — CENTRE FOR EXTRA-SENSORY PERCEPTION, WILL, PURPOSE AND SELF-CONTROL

| | |
|---|---|
| Arteriosclerosis | Refusal to see good – there is much resistance and tension. |
| Loss of balance | Not being centred, and having thoughts that are very scattered. |
| Lower brain | Incorrect beliefs, and the refusal to change old patterns. |
| Dizziness | Refusal to look; not wanting to be here; taking flight and running away. |
| Eyes | Represent your capacity to see clearly. |
| | Far-sighted: fear of the present. |
| | Near-sighted: fear of the future. |
| | Astigmatism: fear of seeing your true self. |
| | Cataracts: not being able to see the future |
| | Cross eyes: seeming to be at cross-purposes; not wanting to see what is out there |
| | Glaucoma: pressure from long-standing hurts; you are overwhelmed and unforgiving. |

|  | Wall-eyed: fear of looking at the present. |
| Ears | What are you wanting to hear? You are not being receptive to life around you. |
| Pituitary gland | This is your central control centre, your will; you may feel that you cannot control your thoughts. |

### 7 CROWN CHAKRA — INNER DEVELOPMENT, UNITY, HIGHER CONSCIOUSNESS

|  |  |
| Brain function | The left side of the brain controls the function of the right side of the body. It has to do with logic, analytical and rational thought, intelligence, language and mathematics; corresponds to the masculine aspect, Yang. The right side of the brain controls the function of the left side of the body. It has to do with understanding, creativity, feeling and intuition; corresponds to the feminine aspect, Yin. |
| Epilepsy | You are unable to accept your ability to be devoted, and feel that you are being forced in life. |
| Fainting | When you faint, you cut off the flow of life. |

It has been my experience over the years, that if you have unresolved conflict, or issues with either of your parents, you can manifest physical problems in two areas:

Father          Left side of the brain; right side of the body; and the head.
Mother          Right side of the brain; left side of the body; and the legs.

There are several different therapies that address the imbalance of the chakras due to emotional/mental patterns: positive thinking, creative visualization and hypnotherapy. All are effective and can be used with Reiki.

Of course, there are many more symptoms that could be mentioned. There are any number of illnesses that involve several chakras. With Reiki, you do not have to know the cause, because the cause is addressed at the same time as the resulting physical problem. This chapter was written to give you more insight into yourself. It is my hope that you have benefited from it.

Wholeness is harmony: a perfect balance between our plus and minus aspects; masculine and feminine; giving and receiving; and being and doing. I believe that in this harmony and stillness, we can experience our souls and our oneness with all things.

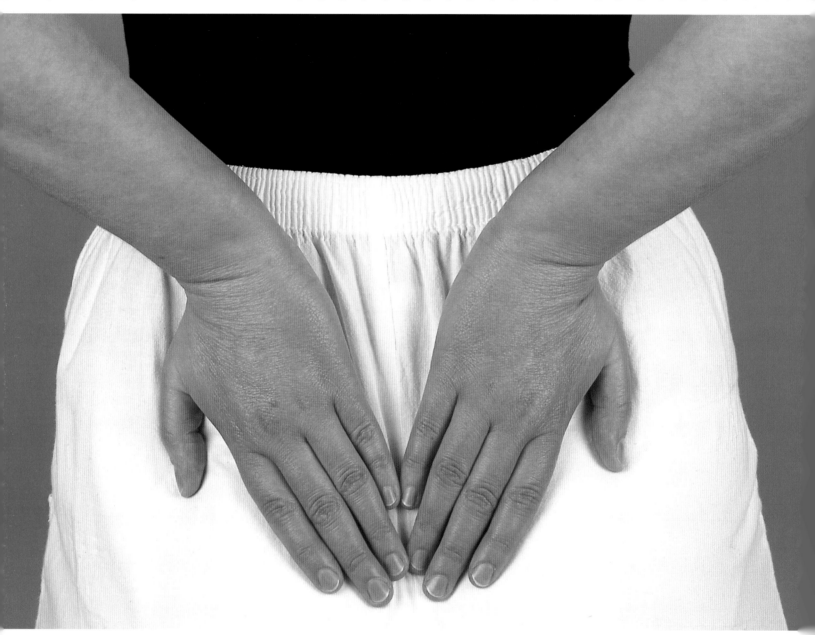

# My Personal Lesson for Living in the Moment, Trusting and Stepping Out in Faith

A few days before leaving the United States in June of 1989, I stopped by to see a friend of mine at her office. As I sat down, an older woman who was sitting there looked at me and said, 'You are going on a long journey very soon, you will no longer live in the United States. Take all that you need, especially warm clothes, because you are going to wake the sleeping people of the churches.' I remember thinking what a strange thing for someone to say to me. I had no intention of working in churches. I was going to take some courses in England so that I would be able to work in a deeper way with people, and I intended to return in three months. I had made the decision to quit my regular job and concentrate on learning more techniques that would help in my work with people. Since I had become a Reiki Master in 1983 I found that I was drawn more and more into service. The changes I was experiencing in myself also led me to make big changes in what I wanted to do and how I wished to live my life.

I had decided in 1980 to take a Reiki course to see if it would help my healing process. I had been told that by the time I was 40 years old I would be completely paralyzed and live my life in a wheelchair.

When I began working with Reiki on myself, I experienced a return to harmony on all levels. My mental and emotional outlook on life was changed dramatically for the better. I was no longer paralyzed and, most important for me, I felt like I had touched my soul and experienced a profound peace. I had returned to my divine nature. So much so that I said I felt as though I had reawakened after a long sleep.

I had no idea how profound the words of that woman would become. I headed off to Europe and my life changed drastically for the better. While I was in England I made the decision to stay in Europe. The people I met there were interested in Reiki and in the message of brotherhood and peace. I was the first Reiki Master in England, so I began travelling and teaching courses and responding to life. Eventually everything I owned in the United States was sold, so there were no material things to hold on to, or go back to. My family was shocked because I, who always had to have the security of a paying job and place to live, just let everything go and began following an inner voice. They did not understand and wondered what would become of me.

I went to work in Scotland with a group of doctors who were interested in the effects of Reiki in clinical application. I also worked with doctors to determine the results of using Reiki with depression, and also the effects of Reiki on motor neurological disorders. It was an exciting time for me to be so involved with Reiki, people and research. Yet, something seemed to be missing and I prayed for a direction to go in, in order to be of service. Life supplied the answer within ten minutes of saying a prayer to be guided to be of service. I was told to go to Czechoslovakia.

I began my journey to Czechoslovakia at the end of January 1991. I left everything behind me again to follow that inner voice. It was my wish to serve and I began this part of my journey by teaching English in the regional hospital and gynamisum in Kolin. I arrived in the then country of Czechoslovakia on February 3, 1991. A friend in Holland had given me her old coat and another

friend had given me a pair of boots. Both were put into use immediately: it was colder than I could ever remember experiencing before.

An opportunity came to teach English in a regional hospital in Kolin. The doctors there were interested in what I had done before I lived in their country. It was an opening for their first experience of Reiki and of the unconditional love that this experience brings. The opportunity to teach Reiki in Czechoslovakia began. In the late spring, I taught the first class to 28 doctors in that district hospital in Kolin.

I have now been travelling and teaching Reiki all over the Czech Republic and Slovakia for the past nine years. There are over 30,000 Reiki students in these areas alone. I have been to Poland, Norway, France, the UK, Austria, Germany, The Netherlands and Greece, and students have come from many parts of the world to take a Reiki course in the Czech Republic. The International Association of Reiki is based in Liberec, there are members from all over the world.

During the time I have been here I have learned so much about myself. I came thinking that I would be of service. I have been and will continue to be. However, the country and the people have also been of service to me. I have had the opportunity to redefine myself, to continue to let go and choose to create in the present moment all sorts of wonderful things. I have also written several books that have been published in several languages.

I see before me churches in every village and town and am reminded of the woman's words 'wake the sleeping people of the churches.' What profound words those seem to me now. The Czech Republic is in the heart of Europe. How important the heart is to the whole organism. How important love is to heal broken hearts. Reiki is the unconditional love of the Universe. If one has a religious philosophy then it can be said that Reiki is the unconditional love of God. Personally, I have felt a reawakening of my own spiritual aspect. In my experience, others feel the same. The spiritual light comes back on and there is certainly more love and light available for us and also for the country as a whole.

I have been asked why I think so many people from the world are drawn here to the Czech Republic and it seems to me that it is becoming a centre of spiritual development. We as a body of people who are deeply spiritual will play an important part in what happens in times to come. In order for that to happen and for us to be of service, we must first reawaken our own spiritual nature and be spiritually strong within ourselves.

Many people who are experiencing their own spiritual reawakening are now finding ways to help others in this waking up process. Certainly that is what I feel that I am doing here. The beautiful message of Reiki enables us to return to our innermost divinity. We are drawn back to our wholeness and in this experience we can, if we choose, also experience our divine nature. When this happens we can then also experience the divinity in others. Light embraces light as it sees past the illusion of darkness.

The fact is that we are all light beings in a process of rediscovering our inherent nature. I have been witness to so many people waking up and seeing their own beauty, to then understand deeply that they make a difference in our world, so that the natural response is to reach out to others in service. It is for this reason that I think the future will be supported by what happens in Europe and certainly what happens in the Czech Republic. When the oldest parts of our culture return to their spiritual divinity, it will then lead the rest of the world by example back into their own return. Where countries and people as a whole who have experienced deep repression throughout centuries now find a way to be empowered individuals and to empower others into their greatness, great changes will naturally take place worldwide. I believe the changes will start here and we will support these changes by remaining clear instruments for love and peace.

My willingness to trust and step out in faith has given me the ability to live my life more fully than I could ever imagine possible. To be of service gives me the greatest joy. I have received a varied education. I have found that the best teacher is life itself. Life teaches me – I see and hear my Creator in all living things, and respond with love.

Come, join me…!

## WHAT IS THE DIFFERENCE?

People have asked me why I chose this country to do my work and what the difference is between Eastern Europe and the West. First of all, I truly believe that the Czech Republic chose me. I responded to the messages I was given and, out of my vision, my work in Eastern Europe started here. It is very hard to put into words what I experience on a daily basis. There are so many sights, sounds and experiences that make up my relationship to this country and its people. The music stirs me to the very depth of my soul. Their songs are sung from deep inside – the oldest memories come to the surface. They sing about love, family, working in the fields and even drinking beer! – but with a joy for life that surpasses anything I have experienced before. I feel their hearts in their songs.

The country is beautiful – in spite of the environmental problems they are experiencing, there is a breathtaking beauty that is present. I love the villages with their own special character and the churches everywhere. It speaks to me of a deep spiritual heritage and a pride in family and accomplishment. They are, as a group of people, independent, loyal, hardworking and fun-loving. They value their families and understand about commitment. They certainly have had opportunity not to believe they have an individual value, but that is changing and, as they value themselves more, others around them will value them likewise. They are innocent – there is a purity and cleanness present in them, as if they are unspoiled. I love seeing their eyes light up, with their spirit shining brightly. They are not afraid of hard work, and, when they decide to learn something, they put their entire being

into the project. Small things are important to them. When they have made friends with someone, they are truly their friends for life. By their conditioning, they have for a long time been a society that does not trust. They did not trust the government, nor their neighbours. They only had their immediate family to be open with. They were taught that they did not really matter. What they thought or did was not important. I see that now they are finding that it does matter what they think and how they feel. They are part of the greater whole. The more they reach out and open up to people, the more there is potential for people to be open with them.

In the West, I find that people generally possess more material things, but that often it is the things that possess them. It has been a psychological game to see who can have more or better, as if that is how your personal value is established. It is by the external things the person owns that a judgement is made about their success or failure. I am not saying that this is true everywhere – but generally. The United States is so large, with many big cities. However, in the smaller communities it is probably not so prevalent. In their rush to develop technologically, people have moved away from the family. People often live so far away from each other that it may be years before the family is together. They move at such a fast pace that there is very little time to enjoy small precious moments. They try to pack more and more into their day. I am speaking out of my own personal experience – I was like many Westerners. We perhaps do not know our neighbours well. On the one hand, we are more friendly at first – we greet people we do not know – so there is a informal attitude in many places. But we have a lot of

acquaintances – and few close friends. In their search to find happiness, they take a lot of courses, but the majority of people are doing the course because it is the newest thing to do, so you hear 'Oh, I have done that' or 'I have been there'. Instead of integrating the material, it is more or less filed away. What is true? For the most part, people in the West know that their voices count, that what they think and how they feel is valued. They are hard-working people. The streets, contrary to belief, are not paved with gold. In most families, the mother and father both work to provide a living for the family. They have a big work ethic. The harder they work, the more they are rewarded. The more input they give to the job, the more they are valued as employees. So, if they are willing to work hard and believe in themselves and their contribution, they will reap greater benefits. People work hard and play hard as well. They are deeply committed to individual rights and the community. There are more and more groups of people coming together to address the environment, ecology and issues of society. They are interested in the world situation.

There are positive and negative aspects in both areas of the world. It seems to me that we can see and experience the polarity, one side having material things, the other not having. The not-having has enabled people to remain close to one other and make the most of everything. Please do not be so quick to reach for the other side. There is a middle road to travel for both the East and West, where I believe we can have our values of family, home, country and ourselves. Be willing to reach into the community and even out into our world. Be comfortable, but ever watchful of waste and the effects of our collective thinking and actions on our

environment. Where we have our family structures, we are open, trusting and see what we share, rather than just our differences. It all involves balance, just as Reiki is about balance. By being in the East, I have had the opportunity to experience the other side of the polarity at a very deep level, and to realize that here there is much more that speaks to my soul. The people here have been great life teachers for me. I am still learning from this country and the people. Here, I am more alive, more aware and happier with myself, and every day I can see and appreciate the smallest things because I have the time to spend with those things.

## WHY US...?

A long time ago, a group of people gathered with a spiritual teacher whom they called Grandmother. One evening, they asked her, 'Grandmother, what has brought us together this time?' She replied, 'We have come together to talk, from our hearts, about ourselves, our families and the problems of the world. We are all equal, and bring much to each other. At the end of the evening we must find our way home, so we reach to the central flame to take a spark of light, in order to light the way. But, remember that, not only do you light the way for yourselves, but you light the way for thousands of others as well. Hold your flame high!'

To all of you who have found this book and read it: there is a reason for our being brought together. We have been on a journey. May you always remember that you

are the light of the world. Hold your personal flame high; show the others the way home to peace, understanding, health and love. I honour your search for the truth and a way to make a difference in our world.

Blessings and love

Mari

# List of Reiki Organizations

For many years, I found it unnecessary to belong to any organization connected with Reiki. However, my students in America, the UK and Holland wanted to join with their brothers and sisters in Czechoslovakia, so we formed the International Association of Reiki. It is a family organization, to support the awakened spirit in us all. The following are a list of the Reiki organizations of which I am at present aware:

International Association of Reiki –
Main Office
Lesni 14
46001 Liberec
Czech Republic
Tel: +42 (048) 271 0512
Fax: +42 (048) 271 0515
E-mail: reiki@pvtnet.cz
Website: www.wisechoices.com

The Reiki Alliance
PO Box 41
Cataldo, ID 83810
USA

The Radiance Technique Association
International Inc.
4 Embarcadero Center, Suite 5123
San Francisco
California 94111
USA

Reiki Touch Master Foundation
PO Box 571785
Houston
Texas 77057
USA

AERP Practitioners Association
27 Lavington Road
Ealing
London W13 9NN
England

(They also have a networking organization called: Reiki Visions, for which the contact person is Paul Dennis.)

There is also an organization called: Reiki Outreach International, of which the founder is:

Mary A. McFadden
PO Box 609
Fair Oaks
California 95628
USA
Tel: (916) 863–1500;
Fax: (916) 863–6464

The organization was formed for the purpose of creating a network of Reiki channels who are united in service to humanity, and to the planet Earth. Using Reiki daily, directing it to different situations and crises in the world, its aim and common purpose is to make a major contribution to world peace and harmony. The International Association of Reiki is the Czech representative.

A Reiki Master does not have to belong to any of these organizations, but they generally do.

# BIBLIOGRAPHY

Arnold, L. and Nevis, S. *The Reiki Handbook*, PSI, 1982.

Baganski, Bodo and Shalila, Sharmon. *Reiki, Universal Life Energy*, Life Rhythm, 1988.

Baganski, Bodo and Shalila, Sharmon. *The Chakra Handbook*, Blue Dolphin, 1991.

Brown, Fran. *Living Reiki: Takata's Teachings*, Life Rhythm, 1992.

Hay, Louise. *You Can Heal Your Life*, Hay House, 1987.

Hay, Louise. *Heal Your Body*, Hay House, 1988.

Horan, Paula. *Empowerment through Reiki*, Lotus Light, 1992.

Johari, Harish. *Chakras, Energy Centers of Transformation*, Destiny Books, 1987.

Lacy, Mary Louise. *Know Yourself Through Colour*, Aquarian Press, 1989.

# FURTHER READING

## *Books*

Arnold, Larry and Nevis, Sandy. *The Reiki Handbook*, Pennsylvania, PSI Press, 1982.

Baganski, Bodo and Sharamon, Shalila. *Reiki Universal Life Energy*, California, Life Rhythm, 1988.

Barnett, Libby and Chambers, Maggie. *Reiki Energy Medicine*, Vermont, Healing Arts Press, 1996.

Brown, Fran. *Living Reiki – Takata's Teachings*, California, LifeRhythm, 1992.

Burak, Marsha. *Reiki Healing Yourself and Others*, California, The Reiki Healing Institute Encinitas, 1995.

Elwood, Don. *Quest for the Light*, Virginia, FMB Publications, 1992.

Eos, Dr Nancy. *Reiki and Medicine*, Michigan, 1995.

Gleisner, Earline F. *Reiki in Everyday Living*, California, White Feather Press, 1991.

Haberly, Helen J. *Reiki, Hawayo Takata's Story*, Maryland, Archedigm Publications, 1990.

Hochhuth, Klaudia. *A Practical Guide to Reiki*, Australia, Gemcraft Books, 1993.

Horan, Paula. *Empowerment through Reiki*, Wisconsin, Lotus Light Shangrila, 1995.

Horan, Paula. *Abundance through Reiki*, Wisconsin, Lotus Light Shangrila, 1995.

Lubeck, Walter. *The Complete Reiki Handbook*, Wisconsin, Lotus Light Shangrila, 1994.

Mackenzie Clay, A. J. *One Step Forward For Reiki*, Australia, The Reiki Teaching Centre, 1992.

Mackenzie Clay, A. J. *The Challenge to Teach Reiki*, Australia, The Reiki Teaching Centre, 1992.

Milner, Kathleen. *Reiki and Other Rays of Touch Healing*, Arizona, Milner Publications, 1994.

Mitchell, Karyn. *Reiki – a Torch in Daylight*, Illinois, Mind Rivers Publications, 1994.

Narrin, JaneAnne. *One Degree Beyond, A Reiki Journey into Energy Medicine*, Washington, Little White Buffalo Cottage, 1998

Petter, Frank Arjava. *Reiki Fire*, Wisconsin, Lotus Light, 1997

Petter, Frank Arjava. *Reiki, the Legacy of Dr. Usui*, Wisconsin, Lotus Light, 1998

Petter, Frank Arjava and Usui, Dr. Mikao. *The Original Reiki Handbook of Mikao Usui*, Wisconsin, Lotus Light, 1999.

Rand, William R. *Reiki, the Healing Touch*, Michigan, Center for Reiki Training, 1991.

Veltheim, Dr John and Esther. *Reiki the Science, Metaphysics and Philosophy*, Pennsylvania, PaRama Publishers, 1995.

# Index

honesty 12–13
hormones 159
hygiene 39
hyperglycaemia/hypoglycaemia
    *see* diabetes & blood sugar
    imbalances
hypothalamus 18, 158, 169
    hand positions affecting 57,
    61, 77

illnesses
    attachment to 125
    by chakra 164–70, 174–82
    emotional causes xvii, 174–83
    as negative energy xv
    as result of imbalance xvii
    *see also* individual illnesses by
    name eg arthritis
imbalance & balance xvi–xviii
    and chakras 158, 162–71
    removing imbalance see self-
    treatment; treating others
    results of imbalance see
    illnesses
immune system stimulation 58,
    78–9, 81, 97, 117
infections 69–70, 81, 88–9, 113,
    117
    *see also* by part of body
    affected eg lungs
initiation by Reiki Master ix, xv,
    xviii, 16–19, 20, 23
injuries 115
    *see also* by part of body
    affected eg head injuries
inscription, on Usui's tombstone
    4–5
International Association of
    Reiki xiii, 22, 196
international organizations *see*
    organizations

intestinal problems *see* digestive
    & intestinal problems
invocations before treatment 40

Japanese calligraphy, for Reiki
    xiv, xiv
jaspis 153
'Just for today, I will let go of
    anger' 10–11
'Just for today, I will let go of
    worry' 10, 11

'Ki', definition xiv
kidney problems 89, 175
kindness 13

lapis lazuli 148
legal considerations of treating
    others 45–6
liver problems 81, 178
low blood pressure 96, 180
lower lymphatic disorders 98
lung & respiratory problems 56,
    63, 68, 76, 81, 87, 100–3,
    178–80
lymphatic disorders 61–3, 80,
    98–9

malachite 149, 151
mani pura *see* solar plexus
    chakra
massage tables 38
Masters of Reiki *see* Reiki
    Masters
meditation 26–7, 154–5
menstrual problems 66, 80, 84,
    176
mental release technique
    134–5
metabolism problems 58,
    78–9

migraines & headaches 56–7,
    59–60, 66–7, 69–70, 76–7,
    80, 84–6, 88, 96
milk quartz 147
mucus accumulation 64, 82–3
muladhara *see* root chakra
music, playing during treatment
    40
musical notes (tones), and
    chakras 139, 140
nervousness 58, 68, 78–9, 87
nosebleeds 59–60, 85

obsidian 154
oedema 89
oneness & harmony 24–7, 40,
    183
orange 140, 141, 142
organizations
    addresses 196–7
    International Association of
    Reiki xiii, 22, 196
    Radiance Technique
    Association 6, 196
    Reiki Alliance xiv, 6, 196
    Usui Reiki Ryoho Gakkai 2
organs of the body, location 52–3
ovaries *see* sexual glands

pain, sensitivity to recipient's
    48–9, 50
parathyroid glands 52, 158, 161
    hand positions affecting 58,
    67, 78–9, 86
parents
    giving Reiki to children 126,
    128
    unresolved conflicts with 183
payment & fees 46
permission to treat 46–8, 134
Petter, Frank & Cheetna 2